WWDILLUSTRATED

WWDILLUSTRATED

1960s – 1990s

MICHELE WESEN BRYANT

FAIRCHILD PUBLICATIONS, INC.   NEW YORK

Executive Editor: Olga T. Kontzias

Assistant Acquisitions Editor: Carolyn Purcell

Editor: Sylvia Weber

Associate Production Editor: Elizabeth Marotta

Director of Production: Priscilla Taguer

Editorial Assistant: Suzette Lam

Copy Editor: Donna Frassetto

Copyright © 2004

Fairchild Publications, Inc.

Library of Congress Catalog Card Number: 2002108014

ISBN: 1-56367-273-1

GST R 133004424

Printed in Singapore

Contents

Preface

by Howard Kissel

In 1967 *Esquire*, then the hippest of American magazines, in a somewhat condescending annual survey of other publications, called *Women's Wear Daily* "only for those who have not outgrown their taste for the furthest reaches of camp." A mere four years later, however, in 1971, *Esquire* considered *WWD* "the last publication in America edited for an elite audience." If you consider yourself part of America's elite, *Esquire* declared, you should be reading *WWD*.

In its heyday, the readership of *WWD* included not just the garment manufacturers for whom it was originally intended, but also the women whom the most sophisticated designers in New York, Paris, and London were dressing. Before long other publications regarded *WWD* as the bellwether, not just of fashion, but also of more general trends. In the early seventies, for example, the publisher of a dictionary wrote to *WWD* to acknowledge the publication's usefulness in tracing new usages in the American language.

One of the assumptions on which *WWD* rested in those days was that its readers had educated eyes. Not only were readers attuned to nuances in American prose, they could read fashion sketches with equal facility. As a result, *WWD* maintained a staff of fashion illustrators that was the equivalent of any season's lineup of the New York Yankees.

One of the remarkable things about the illustrations in this book is not just the power and beauty of work that was intended to be essentially functional, but the fact that each artist was allowed to have his or her own unmistakable style. The assumption was that the elegant idiosyncrasies of the artists would not impede the reader from gaining the necessary information. It was an aesthetic as well as a reportorial experience. By the nineties, however, illustration played a far less integral role in *WWD*.

This book, then, is the record of a golden age in fashion illustration. It is, of course, a chronicle of changing designs, but it is of equal fascination as a document about an art being practiced at its highest level.

"This paper doesn't have to be boring. Fashion is filled with colorful characters. Some of them are real loons. Fashion is fun and the paper should be fun. It should be colorful and visual and controversial and amusing and it should wake people up and keep them awake."

John Fairchild (1960)

Introduction

Since the publication of its first edition in 1911, *Women's Wear Daily* has long been considered the bible of fashion. From 1960 to 1991, illustration was prominently featured in this daily report. Under the aegis of John Fairchild, *WWD* did in fact become more colorful, visual, controversial and amusing than ever before. Fairchild's staff of illustrators was able to capture the spirit of the moment—be it glamour, the space age, naiveté or exotica.

These illustrations are a unique blend of commerce and creativity. Historically, *WWD* has distinguished itself from other fashion publications. Monthly magazines, such as *Vogue* and *Bazaar*, concern themselves with a consumer's fantasy of fashion. In contrast, *WWD* has always covered the business of fashion on a daily basis and with an American point of view. Illustrations and text were geared to Seventh Avenue insiders, who were thought to have an in-depth knowledge of fashion. The Fairchild staff artists worked under tight deadlines and had no time for second-guessing. The artists' initial gut reactions to runway fashions ultimately determined what Americans would and would not adopt as the next latest trend.

The content of their work is also set apart from other fashion art. The *WWD* illustrations were not necessarily meant to sell the fashion, but rather to comment on it and predict consumer reaction. Fairchild's total support of artistic freedom allowed each illustrator to represent a true vision that would have otherwise been compromised in satisfying retail and trade clients. Elsewhere, illustration was eclipsed by photography. From the sixties through the early nineties, *WWD* was the only fashion publication to use illustration on a regular basis. By providing ongoing employment and an opportunity for individual styles to mature and evolve, Fairchild sustained the fashion illustrators who reinvented the art form.

Although *WWD* was readily available by subscription or at specialty bookstores and newsstands in the garment district, beyond Seventh Avenue access was limited. Because each issue of *WWD* had such a short shelf life and an exclusive circulation to the fashion industry, many outside the profession had presumed that fashion illustration died with René Bouché in 1963. The republication of this artwork contradicts that notion and reveals the period following Bouché's death to be, in fact, a boom time for fashion illustration.

From the revolution of the youth cult to the advent of the cyberage, the transformation of the cultural and political climate is detailed in the essays that introduce each decade in this book. The illustrations that follow the text truly capture the artists' personal interpretations of fashion with the changing times. Sadly, over time, much of the original art has been lost or destroyed. Tear sheets from the Fairchild archive have been reproduced in this volume "as is" with tears, creases and ghost images from the flip side. Compositions that were created to accommodate text and ad space have been honored wherever possible. Although amending and deconstructing the artwork was not the objective here, in some instances the layering of compositions in an entirely new context creates the impression of found art. Such rediscovery of the Fairchild illustrators' vision and creativity goes to the true ambition of this book. *WWD Illustrated: 1960s–1990s* is a comprehensive—and long overdue—volume that celebrates the Fairchild artists' contribution to fashion.

ACKNOWLEDGEMENTS

My passion for fashion drawing has been nearly lifelong. By the age of eight, I was a certifiable fashion illustration groupie. I couldn't wait to see the next issue of *WWD*, brought home especially for me by a thoughtful neighbor who worked in the garment center. As a determined and starstruck neophyte in the late seventies, I made it my business to study fashion illustration with the Fairchild staff artists teaching at Parsons School of Design. I can recall many epiphanies along the way. Until I studied with Richard Rosenfeld, I simply could not draw feet. Steven Stipelman showed me how to render navy and black garments without obscuring garment detail. Steven Meisel rightfully accused me of imitating another illustrator's style. His conviction that every illustrator should find their own style was pivotal in my creative development. This book is my way of passing on the baton.

Over the course of my career as a fashion artist and educator, it has been my privilege to know many of the Fairchild artists—first as instructors and later as colleagues at FIT and Parsons. I would like to thank Glen Tunstull for allowing me to interview him. Robert Passantino was especially generous with his time and offered insights based on his

30 year career at *WWD*. I would also like to thank Howard Kissel for his support of this project.

From initial brainstorm to completion of this book, *WWD Illustrated: 1960s–1990s* could have never seen the light of day without the support of my husband, Stan Bryant. Thanks also goes to my parents, Phil and Elayne Wesen, for taking me in tow to the Museum of Modern Art for drawing lessons at the age of five. I am especially grateful to Francesca Sterlacci, chair of the Fashion Design Department at FIT, for facilitating my career in education. Bina Abling's sage advice was invaluable to a new author. Diane DeMers, who is unsurpassed in collegiality, graciously allowed me access to her personal archive of tearsheets. Phyllis Magidson, curator of the costume collection at the Museum of the City of New York, clarified and helped me stick to the facts.

Thank you to the reviewers for their thoughtful suggestions of an extremely rough draft manuscript: Attila Prazsak, Karen Santry, Shirley Kennedy, and Phyllis Tortora.

I would also like to thank many of the people at Fairchild Books who shared my commitment to this project. Merle Thomason, who has been tireless in the maintenance of the Fairchild archive for over 40 years, is a living, breathing search engine. During the course of my research for the images in this book, Merle provided me with much of the anecdotal history that is woven into the text. Elizabeth Marotta, who took on this project as a chaotic work in progress, was enormously helpful in the revision, organization, and production of the book. Adam Bohannon's cover and interior design came as a surprise and a delight. Thank you to Donna Frasetto, who thoroughly copyedited the early stages of this manuscript, and was very insightful. I would especially like to thank Olga Kontzias, who got behind this project early on and gave it her steadfast support through to the finish line.

WWDILLUSTRATED

WWD60s

"For the first time in the history of the world . . . the young are leading us. They are discovering their fashion power just as they are discovering their social and political power. They are bringing about a natural fusion of person and dress . . . for more than three hundred years the French woman has dictated fashion. Now at last, the American woman is coming into fashion maturity, fashion freedom."

Rudi Gernreich (1967)

I n July 1960, John B. Fairchild returned to New York from the Paris bureau to become the publisher of *Women's Wear Daily*. His ambition was to revitalize the content and presentation of the Fairchild family-owned trade publication. He believed that the artwork in *Women's Wear Daily* had to become more daring to generate interest. With John Fairchild as publisher, the collaboration of artists and editors exerted a substantial new influence on the content of *Women's Wear Daily*. He abbreviated the masthead to read *WWD* and assigned Art Director Rudy Millendorf the task of redesigning page layouts to feature less text and larger visuals.

The revitalization of *WWD* corresponded to the fashion industry's parallel break with the past. Starting in 1959, haute couture was redefined and amended with the American concept of ready-to-wear. As women demanded clothing that was more in line with contemporary values and attitudes, *WWD* began to focus on the interesting people and changing lifestyles that influenced fashion. Reporting from Paris in July 1960, John Fairchild had suggested that in their campaign for the presidency, Mr. and Mrs. John F. Kennedy appeared to be running for office on the fashion ticket. He also disclosed Jacqueline Kennedy's need for maternity clothing and her preference for French couture. The Democratic Party was hard pressed to counter Mrs. Richard Nixon's "good Republican cloth coat."

After John F. Kennedy was elected president, the new first lady was required to filter her fashion sensibilities through the more politically correct creations of repatriated European and American designers such as Oleg Cassini and Donald Brooks. In doing so, she came to be known as the prototypical American fashion icon, positioned on the cutting edge of a wave to Americanize fashion. Early on, as a young and fashionable first lady, Kennedy continued to buy French couture on the

sly. *WWD* reported on rumors of clandestine shopping excursions in which her sister Lee Radziwill was used for subterfuge. Nevertheless, with the appearance of a domestic fashion icon in the White House, American ingenuity was increasingly extended to apparel. Kennedy ushered in a decade in which the radical changes in fashion mirrored the revolutionary social and political events of the time.

Although the Americanization of fashion can be credited in part to the influence of Kennedy, other forces were at work. Issues of copyright infringement began to surface in November of 1960, when Christian Dior filed suit against Alexander's, a New York department store, for creating knockoffs of the couture. After a legal settlement was reached, representatives of American department stores continued to attend the couture collections, but for a fee that was later applied to the purchase of original garments and/or muslins. As a result of this new protocol, there was a false economy to knocking off the couture. Bowing to the bottom line, American manufacturers increased their reliance on design services closer to home. By 1963, *WWD* began to champion the work of American designers such as Oscar de la Renta, Bill Blass, and Donald Brooks. Gradually, department stores also stopped the practice of clipping labels out of garments manufactured in the United States.

The fact that American-designed ready-to-wear had come into its own was also due, in part, to the ongoing population explosion that began in 1946. By 1960, more than half the population in the United States was younger than 20 years of age. These baby boomers were the children of middle-class parents who had attained status through consumerism in the years of prosperity following World War II. During this post-war era personal incomes were on the rise and suburbia transformed the American landscape. Everything a family owned including their house, car, furniture,

and clothing symbolized their place in society. The baby boom demographic was responsible for an increase in domestic manufacturing as production levels were raised to satisfy the needs of the burgeoning middle class. By 1966, the business world recognized teenagers as an easily influenced key market demographic. The new youth market had no interest in adopting their parents' dress and lifestyle. Elegance and sophistication in fashion were replaced by a new focus on youth and an alternative "street" aesthetic. Fashion was no longer only for the rich and famous. Design innovation moved from the salon into the street with the proliferation of specialty boutiques aimed at the masses. Ongoing experimentation in these small, specialized retail environments allowed boutique designers such as Betsey Johnson (working for Paraphernalia), Norma Kamali, and Stephen Burrows to respond immediately to consumer fads accelerated by the media. As a result, they garnered new respect from the fashion establishment as avant-garde designers.

Bewildered parents of the youth cult were no match for their children in the conflict between the generations. The invention of the television and the atomic bomb separated the boomer generation from all others that came before. Legalization of oral contraceptives in 1965 widened the generation gap as "the Pill" triggered a sexual revolution and Women's Lib . The sixties' youth cult confidently challenged social and political conventions with a blatant disregard for authority. The sheer numbers of the middle class and the rebellion of the baby boomers contributed to the decline of cultural elitism and the success of ready-to-wear. A new kind of anti-snobbery prevailed, and outlandish and eccentric clothing was an expression of the rebellion.

With their self-confidence magnified in both the media and the marketplace, an empowered youth cult set off on an idealistic crusade to change the world. Growing student activism helped to galvanize the civil rights movement. In 1964, the Equal Rights Amendment was signed into law as part of President Lyndon B. Johnson's plan for the Great Society. That same year Dr. Martin Luther King, Jr. became *Time* magazine's man of the year and the recipient of the Nobel Peace Prize. The sixties' civil rights movement ultimately triggered a wave of multicultural fashion that would more fully develop in the seventies. Like the fifties' beat generation before them, members of the youth cult went in search of self-discovery on the road. Prompted, in part, by more affordable airfares, travel abroad was becoming the American college student's rite of passage.

As the youth cult gained a more global perspective, the international head-on clash between communism and capitalism sparked a reconsideration of political ideologies. The Cultural Revolution in the People's Republic of

China brought international student attention to the doctrine of Maoism and the Little Red Book.[1] The high-collared, shirt-like Chinese worker jacket made an appearance in the western hemisphere, where it was incorporated into the new unisex fashion. In Germany, avant-garde artwork was becoming increasingly politicized as Eugen Schönebeck and Gerhard Richter painted likenesses of Mao Zedong. The impact of Maoism extended well into the seventies, when Andy Warhol's iconic serigraph defanged Mao by turning him into a superstar.[2] But for Americans in the sixties, the harsh reality of the cold war was very close to home. The conflict between the United States and the Soviet Union nearly reached critical mass in October 1962 when a major confrontation erupted between the two superpowers in the Cuban missile crisis. Only skillful diplomacy in the eleventh hour averted the threat of nuclear war.

The Americans and the Soviets had been competing with each other since the fifties. On October 4, 1957, Soviet scientists launched the first man-made satellite, *Sputnik I*, into orbit around the earth. The space race was on, and the United States was off to a faltering start. By the end of the decade Americans had regained their confidence when the *Apollo 11* astronauts set foot on the moon. But in the early sixties, Americans who had smugly considered science their exclusive province began to re-examine the status of technology. They were determined to show the world what science had achieved in the United States.[3] In 1962, Seattle was home to the Century 21 Exposition, with exhibits such as the giant spire of the Space Needle, a monorail, as well as national and corporate pavilions celebrating global futurism. Two years later, a high level of corporate investment prompted New York City to host a similar world's fair for an unprecedented two-year run.

As a consequence of this preoccupation with

technology, the aesthetics of futurism began to influence all aspects of popular culture. Dating back to the fifties, commonplace objects had been redesigned to satisfy the popular taste for the space age.[4] Science fiction enhanced by special effects became popular through TV programs such as *Star Trek* and films such as Stanley Kubrick's *2001: A Space Odyssey*. Fashion designers Paco Rabanne, Emanuel Ungaro, Bonnie Cashin, and Rudi Gernreich advanced the futurist aesthetic with streamlined geometric silhouettes and the ad hoc substitution of leather, paper, plastic, and metal for fabrication and trim. The cold war combination of spies, girls, and gadgets in popular entertainment made for additional intrigue in the fashion industry. Extremely well-dressed secret agents in *Dr. No, The Avengers,* and *The Man From Uncle* set trends for new "mod" clothing and hairstyles.

New technology brought with it faster communication that, in turn, accelerated the evolution of style. Durability in product design was no longer an issue, and change for the sake of change was the pervasive premise underlying all marketing.[5] Philosophies, products, music, and fashion all became faddish, changing at a fast and furious pace. Although people were physically separated in the new frontiers of suburbia, they were connected as never before by television. Working in tandem with radio and the press, television was responsible for creating superstars. Yves Saint Laurent became the first celebrity designer when he left Christian Dior in 1962 to form his own couture house. The Beatles' 1964 appearance on *The Ed Sullivan Show* initiated the phenomenon of Beatlemania. Not long after, the British invasion brought Twiggy, the first supermodel, to American attention. Rail thin, with outlined eyes and a pale mouth, Twiggy personified the sixties' space-age waif and a new, youthful standard of beauty.

Members of the youth cult enthusiastically embraced the technologies of the day for entertainment. Following a series of dance fads introduced by the success of the twist, New York nightclubs such as the Peppermint Lounge and the Electric Circus began to feature deejays and prerecorded music in lieu of live entertainment. Seeds were planted for the cultural phenomenon of the discotheque in the seventies. On television, the mod nightclub experience was re-created in shows such as *Hullabaloo* and *Shindig*. Unlike the daytime *American Bandstand*, which showcased a single pop tune, these new programs crammed multiple pop music performances into 30 minutes of prime time. With a new visual component, pop music began to inspire and react to futurist fashion. The fast-paced TV programming geared to the youth cult was the precursor of the eighties' MTV.

America's love affair with technology turned out to be as cyclic as fashion, and in the mid-sixties there was a rebound from futurism. By then, the youth cult had developed a consciousness about the environmental consequences of technology

run amok. In 1965, Ralph Nader's exposé, *Unsafe At Any Speed*, outlined dangerous design flaws in American automobiles and became the bible for responsible consumerism. The practice of prioritizing appearance at the expense of safety was called into question. Thereafter, rejection of technology would be integrated into rebellion against the establishment.

As part of the youth cult's new social consciousness, an objection to violence grew out of the sad turn of current events. The assassination of President John F. Kennedy in 1963, and of Senator Robert F. Kennedy and Dr. Martin Luther King, Jr. in 1968 ended the innocence of an entire generation. Escalation of U.S. military involvement in Vietnam and President Johnson's elimination of automatic student draft deferments resulted in widespread anti-war protests. Agitated demonstrators were held at bay by armed police officers and state troopers. Nightly newscasts featured confrontational politics at home and revealed the death and devastation in Vietnam. Americans presented with the first televised war were led to reconsider the meaning of patriotism. In response to the chaotic times, the baby boomers began to look to the familiarity of the past for reassurance. Nostalgia replaced the focus on futurism that had characterized the early sixties. A new interest in metaphysics and the occult replaced the earlier preoccupation with science.

By the end of the decade, the counterculture was becoming a viable alternative to mainstream values and behaviors. The "Summer of Love" was celebrated in 1968, and a year later the Woodstock Music and Art Fair was the largest rock concert in history. Idealistic "hippies" looked backward to nature, and flowers became their symbolic offering for peace and love. In 1960, Harvard psychologist Timothy Leary began to advocate the use of lysergic acid diethylamide (LSD), a then-legal pharmaceutical, as a way to achieve the higher levels of consciousness described in Tibetan Buddhism.

The potency of LSD and other mind-altering drugs put a different spin on the slogan, "Better Living Through Chemistry."[6] With *The Psychedelic Experience*[7] as their manual for transcendence, the hippies began to "turn on, tune in, and drop out." "Tripping" on natural and synthetic hallucinogenic drugs became a socially acceptable and integral part of the counterculture.

In tandem with the period's changing mores and challenges to convention, artists began to question the nature of reality and the parameters of art. Just as the egalitarian youth movement worked to eliminate elitism, the New York pop art movement blurred the distinction between high and low art. Artists such as Claes Oldenburg and Andy Warhol elevated the status of everyday objects by placing them in a new artistic context. Technical skills honed in the commercial art field positioned Warhol for his wildly successful transition to fine art in 1964. Only a year before, he was still accepting freelance commercial art assign-

Roy Lichtenstein
(1923–1997). *Drowning Girl.*
1963. © Estate of Roy
Lichtenstein. Philip Johnson
Fund and Gift of Mr. and
Mrs. Bagley Wright.
Digital Image © The
Museum of Modern
Art/Licensed by SCALA/Art
Resource, NY.

ments. Jasper Johns and Robert Indiana also pushed the boundaries of fine art by painting graphic images such as targets, numbers, and flags. Roy Lichtenstein's paintings formed a new pop art idiom by idealizing melodramatic cartoon images and their graphic reproduction. The incorporation of news photography in Robert Rauschenberg's paintings was a subversion of genre and a reflection of domestic political turmoil. With a small shift in subject matter, the graphic methods of commercial reproduction had become the vanguard of the fine art world.[8]

Op art painting helped to further demystify fine art for the masses. In 1965, "The Responsive Eye," an exhibition at the Museum of Modern Art in New York City, featured the work of artists using the science of vision to scramble perception. In this exhibition, minimalist and abstract painters such as Ad Reinhardt, Josef Albers, and Bridget Riley examined the optical effects of color and pattern. The hallucinogenic canvases of the op art movement mirrored the psychedelic drug experiences that were a bedrock of the hippie counterculture. The search for new forms and means of expression led to efforts that combined different disciplines in the arts. Frank Stella's shaped canvases represented a fusion of sculpture and painting. Another new art form known as spontaneous "happenings" combined the visual and performing arts by using dance, music, and sensory stimulation.[9] In decades to come, the performance art of the sixties would have an enormous impact on multimedia fashion presentations geared specifically for the eye of the camera.

The new focus on fine art for the masses led to a crosscurrent of mutual influences and subversion of genre in the applied arts. Warhol straddled both worlds in his production of paper dresses silk-screened with the iconographic Campbell's soup can. The celebrated Mondrian dress introduced Saint Laurent's interpretation of modern art into haute couture.[10] The streamlined shift was Saint Laurent's canvas and a direct reference to Piet Mondrian's studies of rectangular structures in primary colors. Geometric abstraction was cleverly used as seaming on the color blocked dress to accommodate body contour.[11] The bright colors of pop art manifested in fashion and advertising. Garments were adorned with the British or American flag, logos, and cartoon imagery. Mod fashion borrowed heavily from op art using bold graphics and a wild mixing of patterns in coordi-

Tom Wesselman (1965–1975). *Nude* from the *Great American Nude* series. © Tom Wesselman / Licensed by VAGA, New York, NY Courtesy, © Photographer Geoffrey Clements / CORBIS.

nated separates and hosiery to achieve the "Total Look." As the hippie movement gained momentum, surface and graphic designers drew heavily on surrealism and art nouveau for psychedelic inspiration. The 1966 Aubrey Beardsley show at the Victoria and Albert Museum in London had a huge influence on textile design. Beardsley, along with other aesthetics and decadents from the 1890s, gained new relevance in the sixties as the sexual revolution brought pornography into the mainstream culture. Throughout the rest of the 20th century, blockbuster museum shows would continue to have a major ripple effect on the applied arts.

Sixties' fashion mirrored the cultural revolution in other ways. The development of the miniskirt and less restrictive trapeze silhouettes bore a direct relationship to the shedding of sexual inhibitions. Sexual emancipation prompted many women to reject social mores such as marriage, fidelity, and conventional gender roles. French designer André Courrèges's miniskirts, short A-line shifts, and go-go boots were both futuristic and a throwback to the twenties, when women's suffrage became a reality. In 1960, American designer Norman Norell dictated who would "wear the pants" by featuring culottes in his collection. The following year, he designed a jumpsuit for eveningwear, and by 1964, European expatriate Rudi Gernreich created a sensation with his topless bathing suit.

As women sought new freedoms in society, they began to spurn the restricting foundations required by earlier fashion dictates. Women protesting the 1968 Miss America Pageant symbolically tossed bras, girdles, and nylons in the trash. Fewer and less structured undergarments permitted the freedom of movement required for the active lifestyles of the sixties. Cumbersome garter belts and panties were replaced by the modern panty girdle.[12] New

Drawing by Kenneth Paul Block
Wireless Fairchild News Service®

Robert Rauschenberg.
Retroactive I. 1963.
Courtesy, WADSWORTH
ATHENEUM, HARTFORD. Gift
of Susan Morse Hilles.
Reprinted with permission.

brassieres were designed to make a fashion statement with little regard for actual support and shaping. New fiber technology dovetailed with Women's Lib to facilitate the invention of panty hose, the "no bra" bra, and timesaving permanent press fabrics.

The egalitarian youth movement and a booming middle class prompted more and more people to become involved in both warm and cold weather sports. Performance clothing became a new and important market category. Before the invention of technical apparel, winter sports enthusiasts were limited to army/navy surplus for protection from the elements. Off the slopes, however, the military look was more popular than ever. Inspired by the Beatles' Edwardian costumes, featured on the cover of their 1967 album, *Sergeant Pepper's Lonely Hearts Club Band,* military surplus and denim became the fashionable uniform of the nonconformist. Trench coats, flight suits, and sailor pants were all adapted for fashionable civilian use. Utilitarian features such as epaulets, self-belts, fatigue pockets, and grommets were incorporated as design elements into both couture and ready-to-wear garments.

Military looks were only one facet of a much larger fashion direction. Unisex looks evolved as a response to women's expanded role in society. The beauty parlor and the barbershop converged and pioneers of the five-point precision haircut, such as Vidal Sassoon and Paul McGregor, developed a cult following in salons patronized by both men and women. Saint Laurent revolutionized women's fashion by introducing new elements such as pantsuits, tuxedos, and safari jackets borrowed from men's wear.[13] In 1966, Geoffrey Beene established his signature reference of the gray flannel suit for eveningwear. Women began breaking existing dress codes in their adoption of pants and men's haberdashery looks. Just as in the twenties, their tongue-in-cheek affectation of "la garconnes" was deemed appropriate for newly defined gender roles.

Advances in communication technologies caused fashion to trend faster and faster and skirt

J'AI BAISÉ TA BOVCHE
IOKANAAN
J'AI BAISÉ TA BOVCHE

Aubrey Vincent Beardsley, *Salome with the Head of John the Baptist*, 1894.
Courtesy © *Historical Picture Archive/CORBIS*.

hemlines in the sixties fluctuated wildly. Early in the decade, the mini reflected the focus on futurism and emancipation. The midi, popular from 1965 through 1968, suited the nostalgic, rural, and bohemian sensibilities of the hippie movement. By the end of the decade, the addition of the ankle-length maxi resulted in total fashion anarchy. In 1968, Norell featured all three skirt lengths as well as pants in his collection. Although Americans generally preferred the maxi, Europeans were predisposed to the midi, initiating what came to be known in *WWD* as "the longuette" hemline controversy.

While documenting the radical changes of the sixties, the fashion art in *WWD* began to mirror the revolutionary and cross-pollination in the arts. Taking their cue from pop art, *WWD*'s fashion illustrators began to break the conventional rules of design with an eye to attracting attention and expanding on the text. The illustrations became edgier, and now included nudity and suggestive content. There was a presumption of intellectual sophistication in references to fine art, literature, and film. A new, elongated figure proportion corresponded to the younger, androgynous standard of beauty. Contour drawings and the elimination of halftone reflected the growing art nouveau trend. Brush, rapidograph, and felt-tip pen were used to create a single, continuous line that defined mass. The selective omission of details was also definitive, forcing the viewer's eye to fill in the blanks. The relationship among art, text, and photography changed as technology evolved. Because the illustrations in *WWD* were not typeset, they required a different reproduction technology from that used for the text. More often than not, the *WWD* illustrators were faced with the challenge of filling an irregular space left by the text.[14] Instead of being an obstacle, L shapes became a springboard for innovative layouts.

Although photographic and televised images were everywhere, the artist still had the edge over

the camera in the sixties. Photography was thought to deliver the straight goods, lacking the bias and exaggeration found in illustration. Moreover, studio shoots were expensive and required a long lead time. Drawings, on the other hand, could be done on short notice and adjusted to accommodate the limitations of "wireless" transmission. In the sixties, couture presentations were exclusive, invitation-only affairs, and the latest designs were closely guarded secrets. Leaking information prior to the collections was considered both industrial espionage and a scoop. If a photographer could not gain access to the collections, he or she was at an impasse. An artist, however, could work from anecdotal information and speculation, fudging the details as necessary. Relying on real and imagined observations, the fashion artist could create a flattering fiction. Commenting on his long career at *WWD*, artist Steven Stipelman admitted that although he regularly attended the French collections,

"Seventy percent of the work I did was of clothes I'd never seen." His understanding of individual design philosophies enabled him to visualize forthcoming fashion trends.[15]

Although newly hired artists would reliably imitate Kenneth Paul Block (Kenneth), the leading illustrator at *WWD*, no one drawing style dominated this publication in the sixties. Experimentation led to the emergence of distinct illustration styles in the work of Analiese, Pedro Barrios, Julianne Engelman, Jack Geisinger, Sandra Leichman, Antonio Lopez (Antonio), Dorothy Lovarro, Robert Melendez, Richard Rosenfeld, Stipelman, and Richard Thornton. The inclusion of an illustration credit line, beginning in 1960, underscored the value of the artists' contributions.

By JOHN B. FAIRCHILD
Wireless Fairchild News Service®

PARIS. — Those smart and charming Kennedys — Jacqueline, wife of the Senator, and his mother, Mrs. Joseph P., are running for election on the Paris Couture fashion ticket.

The Kennedys are not enough anti-American-fashion to make a Republican campaign issue, but the French Couture ranks both as among the biggest United States private customers who pay nothing less than $350 and on up into the thousands for a Paris couture model.

Together, the two Kennedys spend an estimated $30,000 per year for Paris clothes and hats—more than most United States professional buyers.

Like all good Democrats and Republicans, Jacqueline Kennedy once bought models on sale at Jacques Griffe.

Jacqueline is in the avant garde, while her mother-in-law "is more conventional." In the eyes of the Paris couture, both Kennedys dress "well" but "Jacqueline is really elegant"—about the biggest compliment a Paris designer dare pay his customers.

THEY BOTH have been buying with the election in mind. Tall Mrs. Joseph P. has stressed "nothing which will be too noticed—always discreet."

She is down on the couture books as a "faithful twice-a-year

See KENNEDY, P. 5, This Sect.

PARIS BUREAU

These are the latest Paris couture models ordered by Mrs. John F. Kennedy from Gres. Mme. Gres did not design these models specifically for maternity wear, but the slim Jacqueline Kennedy will be able to wear the loose silhouettes for a while. Delivered to her recently, the clothes were ordered by the Senator's wife from sketches.

Two-piece dress, left, is composed of water green silk middy top and skirt in yellow wool etamine.

Loose reversible coat, right, in turquoise brushed woolen, has wide cuffs in the white reverse side of the fabric.

Additional Gres styles ordered by the wife of the Presidential aspirant appear on page 5, along with reports on her fashion preferences.

Fashionable Kennedys Big Paris Customers

In the beginning of the sixties, Kenneth Paul Block (Kenneth) was working within

the conventions of fashion art as previously established by artists such as René

Bouché, Carl Erickson (Eric), and René Bouët-Willaumez.

These Designers Made 50

Years of Fashion History

Women's Wear Daily published its 50th anniversary issue in July 1960. In this two-page spread, the attitude of the women portrayed is sophisticated and mature. The figures have a formal stance, and there is an economy of impressionistic charcoal lines. The technique of direct drawing does not allow for revision, requiring both spontaneity and accuracy, and reveals Kenneth Paul Block (Kenneth) as a virtuoso draftsman from the start.

AMERICA'S MR. G.

IN AMERICA, IT'S THE BIG TWO — Mr. N. and Mr. G. Today, James Galanos is one of the world's greatest fashion designers. His influence is fantastic. (Last year's sweater dress is one of the most copied ideas in the fashion world.) Galanos toys with the idea of going to Paris and if he should Balenciaga, St. Laurent and Givenchy would welcome him to their ranks.

THE IMPORTANT GALANOS TRENDS on the same wave length as Europe—the elaboration of the casual look . . . easy silhouettes . . . clean, spare, with one dash of detail — a new series of woolens inspired by the old tennis dress, now for dinner and evening: Simple, naked, effortless — the black dress with very open decolletage, getting away from the high bateau — all evening dresses approached with casualness foremost — easy tailored look — never bouffant or ball gownish.
Top row, from left:
OPEN AIR SUIT in spongy beige tweed — longer jacket — nutria scarf tucked in neckline — double pleat Pantskirt.
OPEN AIR SUIT with shaped jacket (no darts, seams) in camel hair — Pantskirt.
NAKED EVENING LOOK with newly-gathered sleeves, shoulders — body overblouse — black shell pattern matelasse.
NATURAL EVENING DRESS with low back, Pantskirt pleats at back in silver damask.
Below:
SWEATER SLIP in wool jersey — the bare minimum look for evening.
LONG JACKET DINNER SUIT in Bianchini window pane plaid — jacket shaped without seams or body darts.
CASUAL EVENING LOOK for dinner and theater — sweater-cut tweed jacket, tweed

SURPRISE: Boy-tailored suit, feminine fabric (a bed of flowers, printed on Staron's new "Machicoulis," textured, c o o l, porous) — unexpected teamwork by Bill Blass of Maurice Rentner for resort, after.

Drawing by Antonio

In 1962, Antonio Lopez (Antonio) briefly joined the Fairchild staff. At the time, *WWD* was the only publication offering regular employment to fashion illustrators; it was a much-coveted first job. Then, as now, publishers and department stores had policies of exclusivity with contracted artists. Not long after he was hired, Antonio left *WWD* to work for the *Fashions of the Times* supplement at the *New York Times*. He would go on to a prominent freelance career, working for Bloomingdale's, Saks, Missoni, *Vogue*, *Bazaar*, and *Interview*. Antonio's observations about fashion were always imaginatively drawn, using a wide variety of experimental techniques. Each one of "Antonio's girls" established a new standard of beauty.

FAVORITE ENSEMBLE AT BURKE-AMEY THIS SEASON: COACHMAN ENSEMBLE IN BLACK HEAVY CORDED WOOL OTTOMAN (VERRON), WITH A FLASH OF GOLD BRAID ON THE RED LINING. UNDER IT: BLACK WOOL (LESUR) RELAXED DRESS, LIGHTLY TIED IN RED WOOL. SOME PRACTICAL REASONS FOR ITS POPULARITY, ACCORDING TO RONALD AMEY: THE COAT CAN BE WORN FOR LATE DAY, THE DRESS CAN BE WORN TO COCKTAILS ("MUCH MORE ORIGINAL THAN BLACK CREPE").

Drawings by Antonio Lopez

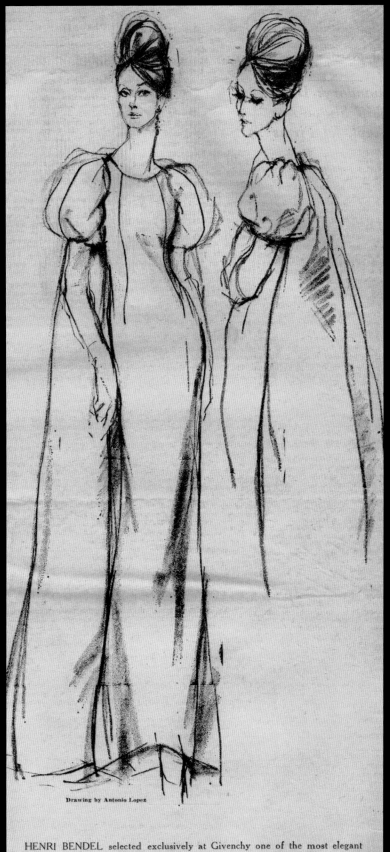

Drawing by Antonio Lopez

HENRI BENDEL selected exclusively at Givenchy one of the most elegant dresses in years . . . Big News: The superb curved seaming (many Givenchy models have multiple seaming) . . . reveals the BeautiFULL BODY . . . captures the whole new look of this Paris Great's masterly curved seaming . . . heralds the return of sleeves and pouffed at that . . . shirrs the back into a flowing cape . . . elegantly perfect for Bendel brides.

These examples of Antonio Lopez's (Antonio) early work reflect a more traditional fashion idiom through the expressive use of a charcoal line. Even so, we begin to see evidence of a new flamboyance in both fashion design and illustration.

Drawings by Sandra Leichman

Playtime

on the Riviera

Wanderlust and reduced airfares made travel more commonplace in the sixties. The clothing worn in warm and cold weather vacation spots began to evolve as a separate seasonal fashion category. Bridging the gap between winter and spring, resort collections are often more experimental in nature. In this illustration, Sandra Leichman documents a new, playful lifestyle in a composition that seamlessly integrates photography, typography, and drawing.

Like all members of the haute couture, Saint Laurent was both serviced and sabotaged by the press. If he received a bad review, he would bar the offending journalist from attending his next collection. In 1965, Saint Laurent insisted that buyers preview his collection first, before the press. Because he was regarded as the most revolutionary designer of his time, the secrecy surrounding Saint Laurent's latest brainstorms piqued public interest. Jack Geisinger had to rely on rumor and speculation to illustrate the much-anticipated Mondrian collection.

imilarly, Kenneth Paul Block (Kenneth) regularly traveled overseas, but with no guarantee of actually being able to attend the collections. His real and imagined observations are indistinguishable; we can never know exactly what he saw. We marvel at his artistry in this illustration of the Kiss Kiss dress (*left*). In 1966, Saint Laurent drew inspiration from pop art by reinterpreting Wesselmann's *Great American Nude* series as engineered surface designs on body-hugging silhouettes. The collaboration of fashion designer and painter was not new; Saint Laurent carried on a tradition begun by surrealists Elsa Schiaparelli and Salvador Dali.

These drawings, transmitted by wireless radio photo, reveal the graphic limitations of early communication technologies. Note the absence of continuous tone and Kenneth's idiosyncratic line work.

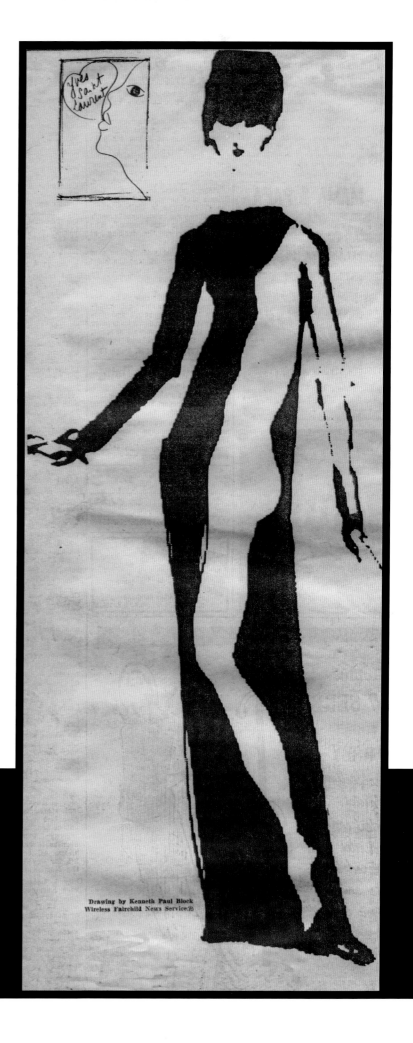

Drawing by Kenneth Paul Block
Wireless Fairchild News Service®

Influenced by Women's Lib and the youth cult, the poses and proportions of the fashion figure began to change in the sixties. The new "superwoman" had an attenuated figure, and the appearance of a natural body freed from restricting undergarments. The poses reflect a shedding of inhibitions elsewhere in society. These kinetic gestures illustrate Ungaro's futuristic trapeze silhouettes that have been designed to allow freedom of movement. In this illustration, Kenneth Paul Block (Kenneth) disregarded perspective by placing smaller figures in the forefront. The overall composition shows the influence of popular poster art from the period.

THE faster than a speedin more powerful than look! up in the sky it's...

SUPERWOMAN
...ullet...
...ocomotive...
...t's a bird, it's a plane,
UNGARO

UNGARO IS THE TERRORIST

His collection was severely criticized by some buyers. They missed the point. But Lord & Taylor saw it:

UNGARO IS GREAT FOR SPORTSWEAR

Certainly the trend to nudity is a natural for sportswear. Sun-tanned bodies look wonderful on the beach. Ungaro shows the Shortest Skirt yet — almost a loin cloth — snapped on, snapped off — and little pants underneath.

IT'S COUTURE SPORTIVE

For those who are young and not a bore. Women will fall for it quickly because they become Superwomen. And this is something they have long waited for. Ungaro's Superwoman is tall, athletic, muscular, sun-bronzed, slightly terrifying. Ungaro's geometric designs are accentuated by bold colors — pink and orange with turquoise, blue and green with red outline, blue ovals with green — in strikingly bright checks, stripes and jacquard patterns. Here are some of his best sellers.

UNGARO LAUNCHES THE SUPERWOMAN
—PARIS BUREAU

THE
CHAIN
GANG

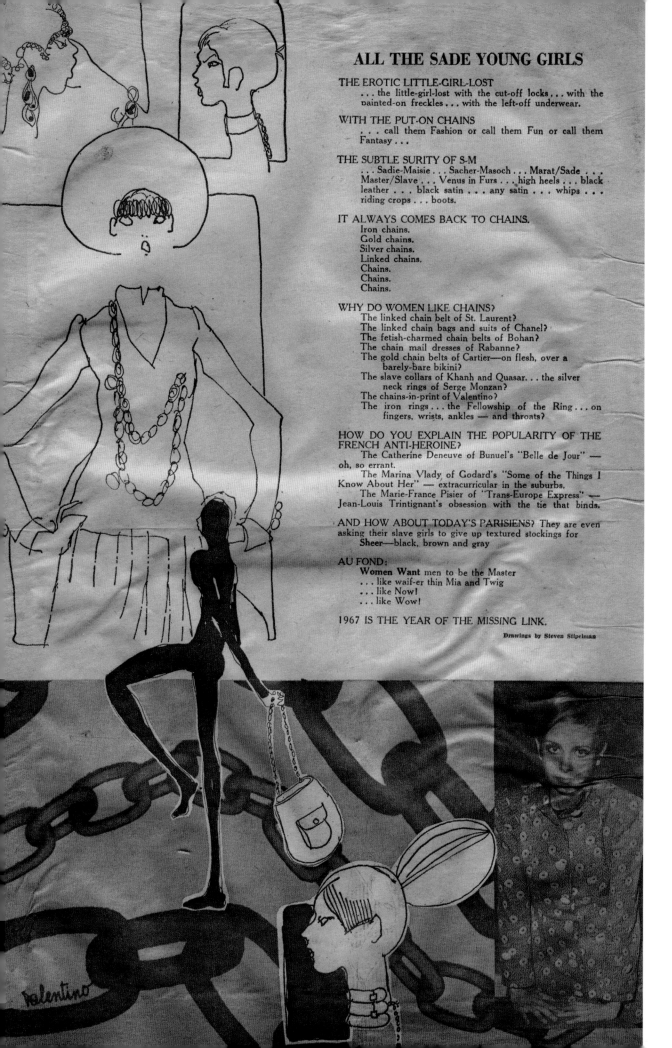

ALL THE SADE YOUNG GIRLS

THE EROTIC LITTLE-GIRL-LOST
... the little-girl-lost with the cut-off locks ... with the painted-on freckles ... with the left-off underwear.

WITH THE PUT-ON CHAINS
... call them Fashion or call them Fun or call them Fantasy ...

THE SUBTLE SURITY OF S-M
... Sadie-Maisie ... Sacher-Masoch ... Marat/Sade ... Master/Slave ... Venus in Furs ... high heels ... black leather ... black satin ... any satin ... whips ... riding crops ... boots.

IT ALWAYS COMES BACK TO CHAINS.
Iron chains.
Gold chains.
Silver chains.
Linked chains.
Chains.
Chains.
Chains.

WHY DO WOMEN LIKE CHAINS?
The linked chain belt of St. Laurent?
The linked chain bags and suits of Chanel?
The fetish-charmed chain belts of Bohan?
The chain mail dresses of Rabanne?
The gold chain belts of Cartier—on flesh, over a barely-bare bikini?
The slave collars of Khanh and Quasar ... the silver neck rings of Serge Monzan?
The chains-in-print of Valentino?
The iron rings ... the Fellowship of the Ring ... on fingers, wrists, ankles — and throats?

HOW DO YOU EXPLAIN THE POPULARITY OF THE FRENCH ANTI-HEROINE?
The Catherine Deneuve of Bunuel's "Belle de Jour" — oh, so errant.
The Marina Vlady of Godard's "Some of the Things I Know About Her" — extracurricular in the suburbs.
The Marie-France Pisier of "Trans-Europe Express" — Jean-Louis Trintignant's obsession with the tie that binds.

AND HOW ABOUT TODAY'S PARISIENS? They are even asking their slave girls to give up textured stockings for **Sheer**—black, brown and gray

AU FOND:
Women Want men to be the Master
... like waif-er thin Mia and Twig
... like Now!
... like Wow!

1967 IS THE YEAR OF THE MISSING LINK.

Drawings by Steven Stipelman

The sexual revolution, launched by the invention and legalization of the birth control pill, had a great impact on the American media. Previously censored explicit sexual content began to appear in mainstream periodicals, film, and art. The publication of Henry Miller's *Tropic of Cancer* in 1961 ended its 30-year ban in the United States. In 1962, Stanley Kubrick's film *Lolita* was released. It was based on Vladimir Nabokov's novel about a middle-aged man infatuated with a teenage girl. The movie kicked off a decade in which the standard of beauty for women would change from adult sophisticate to youthful nymphet.

Stephen Burrows   Jimmy Valkus

The Real Story of 'O'

The sixties saw the advent of new retailing and design concepts aimed at the masses. Avant-garde designers such as Stephen Burrows and Bonnie Cashin began using grommets, dog leashes, and luggage hardware for closures in garment design.

This illustration hints at the illicit activities that were part of the "happening" scene in the sixties. The poses are a departure from static fashion cliché. Drawing and photography are combined to create a surreal effect. The tongue-in-cheek headline references the erotic novel by Pauline Reage.

THE LEATHER MENAGERIE

Dorothy Lovarro's illustration demonstrates how this more youthful appearance was achieved. High-crown bouffant coiffures dwarf tiny faces; bangs frame wide, outlined eyes and pale lips; short trapeze dresses and skirts elongate legs. All of these features are designed to create a more childlike appearance.

High boots and patterned hosiery were an integral part of the "total look." By 1965, the woolen tights prominently featured in Courrèges's futuristic collection were replaced with nylon panty hose. Julianne Engelman's illustration has a painterly quality reminiscent of expressionism. Bold, fluid lines in the illustration by Marilyn Novello (*opposite*) reference art nouveau. Both of these drawings precede the flattened, more decorative style of illustration that became popular later in the decade.

HIGH KICKS

With the incorporation of words and messages into both the garment and pictorial structure, this illustration recalls the word art of dadaism and the arts and crafts movement. Such word images anticipate the popularity of graffiti in the punk movement of the seventies.

THE ART OF LOVE . . .

The message of the doves and the Flower People . . . translated onto the leg by the McCallum Boutique. The Love Tight is opaque . . . seamed up both sides of the leg . . . orange in front with handpainted orange love-lettering on white in back.

Photos by Nick Machalaba

Drawing by Richard Rosenfeld

H ired in 1968, Richard Rosenfeld was one of the first *WWD* artists to reform fashion's visual language. His innovative compositions reflect the synthesis of the arts that evolved in the sixties. In this illustration, photography is incorporated into the illustration as montage. The transparent "no-bra" bra, one of Gernreich's many liberating inventions, was the perfect undergarment for the idealized child-woman—just the other side of puberty.

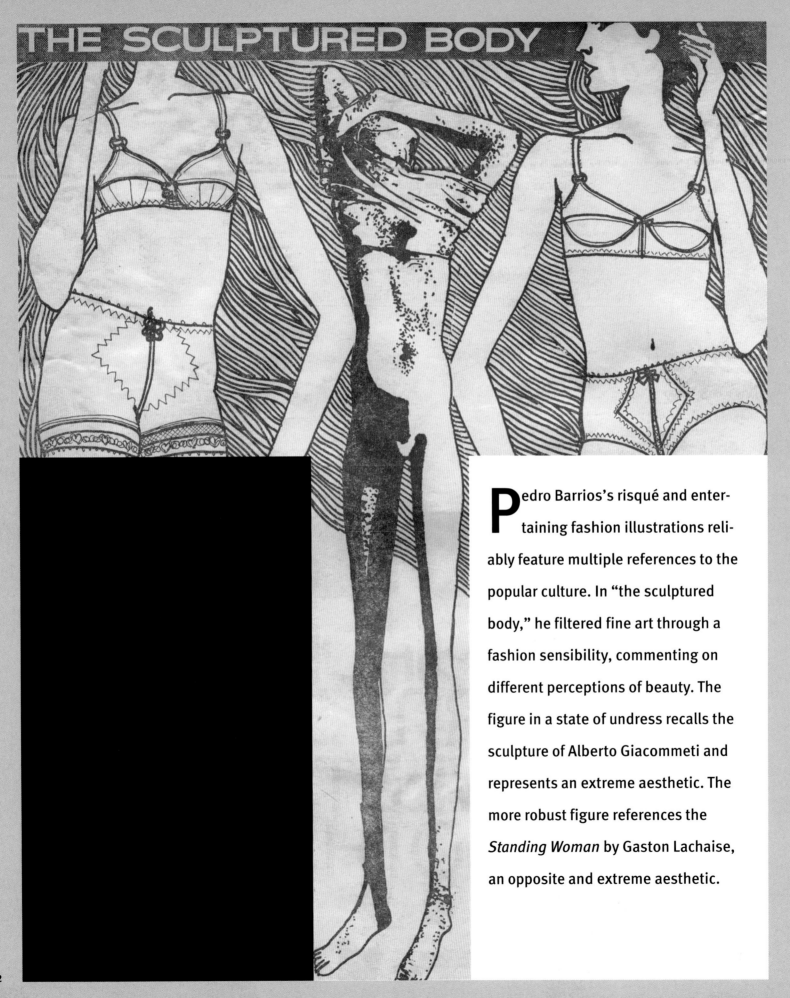

Pedro Barrios's risqué and entertaining fashion illustrations reliably feature multiple references to the popular culture. In "the sculptured body," he filtered fine art through a fashion sensibility, commenting on different perceptions of beauty. The figure in a state of undress recalls the sculpture of Alberto Giacommeti and represents an extreme aesthetic. The more robust figure references the *Standing Woman* by Gaston Lachaise, an opposite and extreme aesthetic.

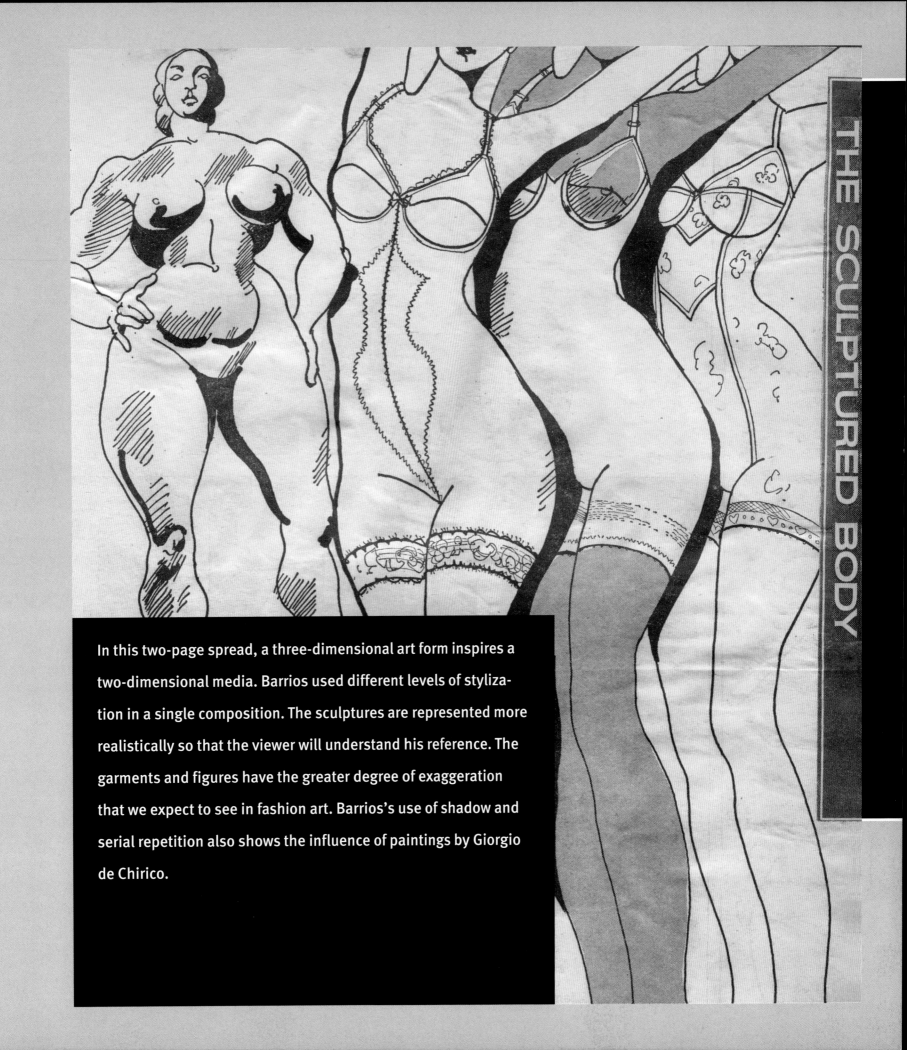

In this two-page spread, a three-dimensional art form inspires a two-dimensional media. Barrios used different levels of stylization in a single composition. The sculptures are represented more realistically so that the viewer will understand his reference. The garments and figures have the greater degree of exaggeration that we expect to see in fashion art. Barrios's use of shadow and serial repetition also shows the influence of paintings by Giorgio de Chirico.

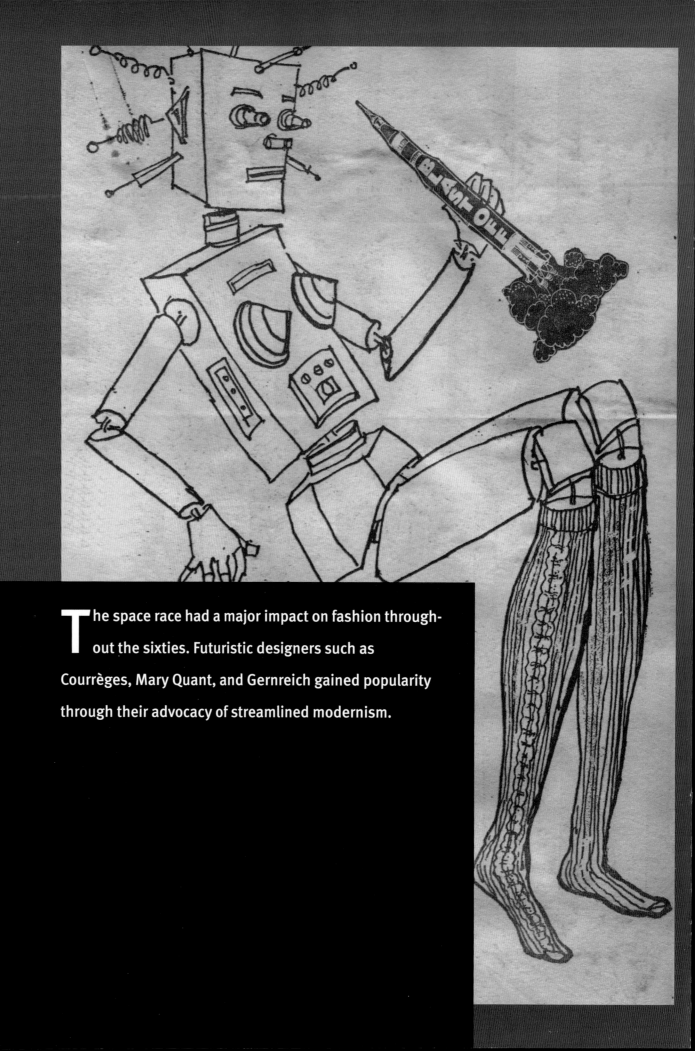

The space race had a major impact on fashion throughout the sixties. Futuristic designers such as
Courrèges, Mary Quant, and Gernreich gained popularity
through their advocacy of streamlined modernism.

XXI

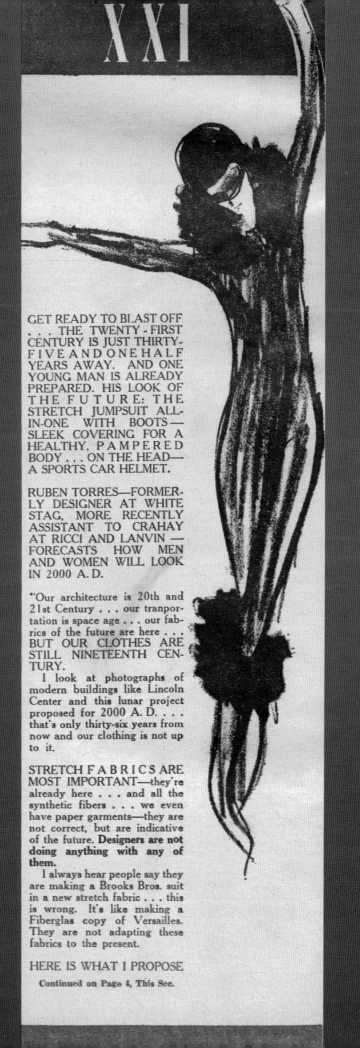

GET READY TO BLAST OFF
. . . THE TWENTY - FIRST
CENTURY IS JUST THIRTY-
FIVE AND ONE HALF
YEARS AWAY. AND ONE
YOUNG MAN IS ALREADY
PREPARED. HIS LOOK OF
T H E F U T U R E: T H E
STRETCH JUMPSUIT ALL-
IN-ONE WITH BOOTS —
SLEEK COVERING FOR A
HEALTHY, P A M P E R E D
BODY . . . ON THE HEAD—
A SPORTS CAR HELMET.

RUBEN TORRES—FORMER-
LY DESIGNER AT WHITE
STAG, MORE RECENTLY
ASSISTANT TO CRAHAY
AT RICCI AND LANVIN —
FORECASTS HOW MEN
AND WOMEN WILL LOOK
IN 2000 A. D.

"Our architecture is 20th and
21st Century . . . our tranpor-
tation is space age . . . our fabrics of the future are here . . .
BUT OUR CLOTHES ARE
STILL NINETEENTH CEN-
TURY.
I look at photographs of
modern buildings like Lincoln
Center and this lunar project
proposed for 2000 A. D. . . .
that's only thirty-six years from
now and our clothing is not up
to it.

STRETCH F A B R I C S ARE
MOST IMPORTANT—they're
already here . . . and all the
synthetic fibers . . . we even
have paper garments—they are
not correct, but are indicative
of the future. **Designers are not
doing anything with any of
them.**
I always hear people say they
are making a Brooks Bros. suit
in a new stretch fabric . . . this
is wrong. It's like making a
Fiberglas copy of Versailles.
They are not adapting these
fabrics to the present.

HERE IS WHAT I PROPOSE

Continued on Page 4, This Sec.

YVES' LITTLE GIRLS

Sketched left to right:

THE NAUGHTY SUNNER . . . ruffled black cotton two-piece sunsuit bordered in yellow.

THE BEACH DRESS . . . red and white gingham belted and bowed at the waist.

THE BLOOMER GIRL . . . in red and white gingham.

THE BABY DRESS . . . black and white gingham with rickrack and ruffles.

—PARIS BUREAU

• Drawings by Kenneth Paul Block

In 1967, the cultural phenomena of the nymphet was combined with space-age sensibilities. In Roger Vadim's film *Barbarella*, Jane Fonda is featured as a sci-fi sex kitten. Film and fashion had increasingly mutual influences. Historical movies featured period costume designs filtered through the lens of sixties' fashion trends. Couturiers returned the favor by designing costumes for film (e.g., Paco Rabanne for Jane Fonda in *Barbarella*, Givenchy for Audrey Hepburn in *Breakfast at Tiffany's*, and Saint Laurent for his muse, Catherine Deneuve, in *Belle De Jour*.) The youth cult's disregard for authority was evident in films such as *Bonnie and Clyde* which, in turn, inspired the late-sixties trend for gangster fashion.

Kenneth Paul Block's (Kenneth) drawing of the mini pantshirt is a departure from his signature style. The total absence of halftones and use of spontaneous crosshatch pen strokes suggests a manic experimentation.

THE PANTSHIRT

GUNTER TURNS THE SHIRT INTO PANTS and ends up with a Mini Pantshirt . . . and his fashion ingredients of the future . . . short, divided, free. Today in his fall collection at Ginala he shows a half-dozen Pantshirts wrapped up with skirts or coated in the trench fashion.

GUNTER RINGS THE FREEDOM BELLE.

Drawing by Kenneth Paul Block

The popularity of pants and culottes contributed to fashion anarchy at the end of the sixties. Women assumed new positions of power in society and began to break existing dress codes. Steven Stipelman's drawing of soft, flowing pants for eveningwear documents another elimination of social requirements for dress.

Richard Rosenfeld was highly influenced by Katharina Denzinger, whose work graced the covers of *Vogue* and *Harper's Bazaar* in the sixties. This painterly illustration of Courrèges's "city pants" fuses nonobjective and figurative imagery in a flattened, cubist picture plane.

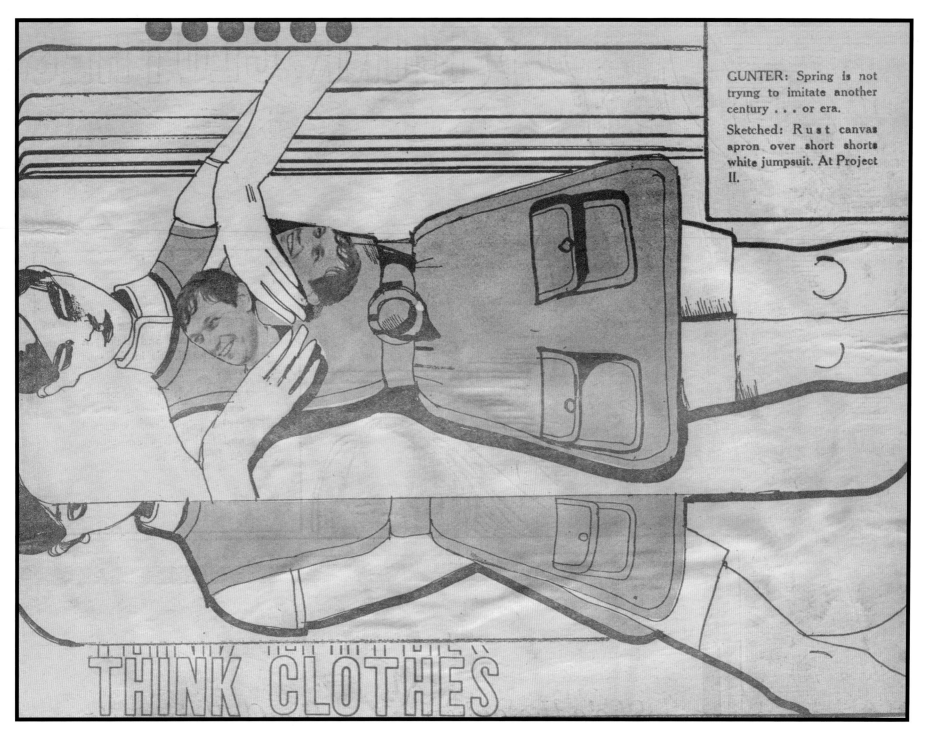

As in many of Rosenfeld's compositions, there is no fixed orientation in this illustration; he literally upends previous fashion clichés. The surrealistic use of photography marks a point of departure from traditional fashion illustration. By artificially manipulating scale, Rosenfeld demonstrates a total disregard for reality. The squircle frame and serial repetition call to mind a TV set with a broken vertical hold. In the sixties, fashion increasingly drew upon film and television as part of a shared cultural experience.

"Estee's eye" (*opposite*) takes on new meaning in Richard Rosenfeld's dreamlike composition. The symbolic imagery of the subconscious, long associated with surrealism, is used to illustrate the latest trends in cosmetics. His irrational mix of photography and illustration specifically references the eye-slashing sequence in the groundbreaking surrealist film *Un Chien Andalou* (1929) by Luis Buñuel and Salvador Dali.

Pop artist Lichtenstein is mimicked in this graphic illustration through the use of a benday dot pattern. The artwork parallels sixties' photography with an extreme point of view used to dramatic effect. Selective foreshortening reproportions the figure to correspond with the new child-woman ideal. As fashion artists left static poses behind, they had to rely on photo references to simulate modern situations and extreme perspective.

PARIS HEADS

To service the growing cosmetic and hair care industries, beauty illustrations began to appear more often in *WWD*. Richard Rosenfeld's signature use of space is disorienting and ambiguous. His composition is an indication of the more ornate aesthetic that developed later in the sixties in tandem with the psychedelic counterculture.

Coco Chanel was one of the first women's wear designers to recognize the appeal of functional apparel when she made trench coats, pea coats and polo coats fashionable in the twenties. Similar currents in sixties' society (e.g., Women's Lib) created a new demand for unisex looks. Military surplus was adopted as the tough chic uniform of the fashionable antiestablishment.

Designer Gernreich predicted that in the future, men and women would dress exactly the same.[16] Androgeny in the sixties translated as women dressing like men. The unisex concept gradually evolved to include feminized looks for men. By the late sixties, fashionable men began to wear jewelry, grow their hair, sport ponytails and carry purses. Seventies "glamrock" would be the epitome of the unisex trend, in which only "real men" had the courage to dress like a girl.[17]

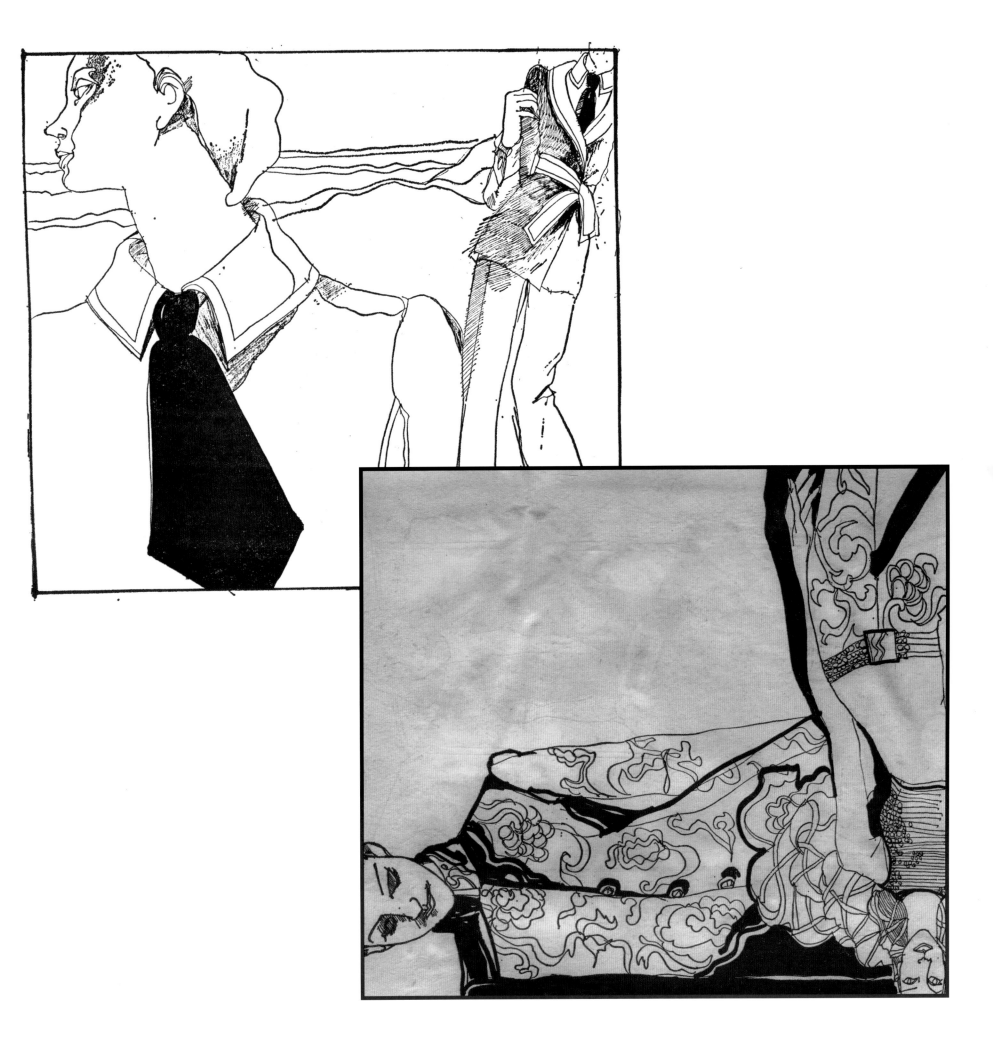

As travel became more affordable, performance apparel developed as a market category for new active lifestyles. Technical clothing offered a chic alternative to army surplus for winter sports. Julianne Engelman's illustration features the graphic representation of a ski slope and figures with a youthful proportion and vitality.

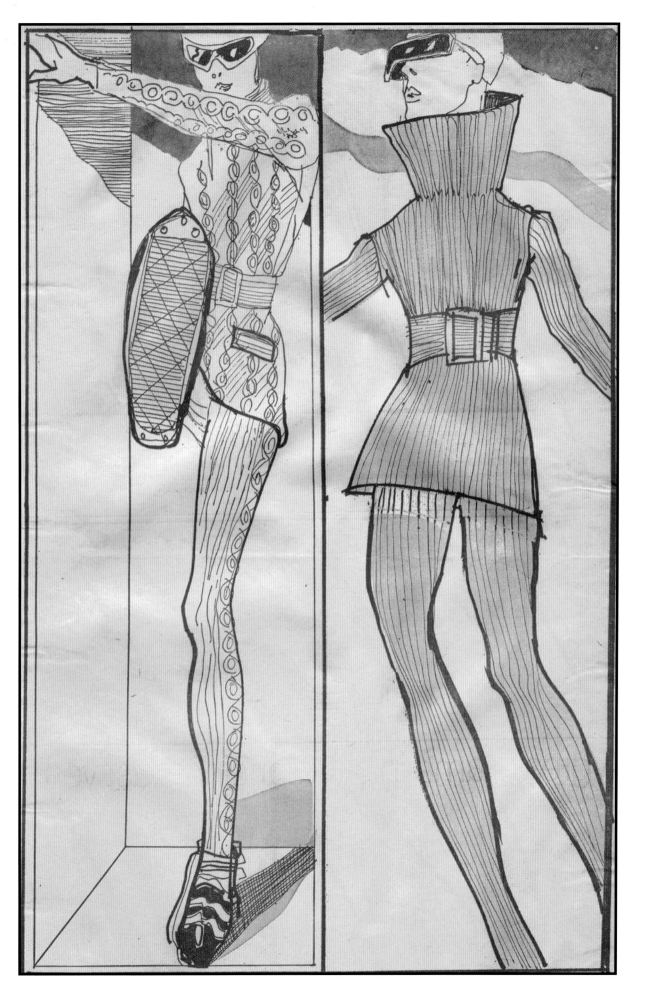

Richard Rosenfeld takes a more surreal approach in his drawing of après-ski tights and tunics. The extreme perspective and accurate representation of the gear in both illustrations suggests the use of photo references and in-depth research.

THE MAXI vs. THE MIDI

THE MAXI v

MIDI VS. MAXI . . . THE FIGHT GOES ON.

In New York it's the maxi . . . on the streets today, but retailers and designers see a definite swing toward the Midi for spring. (WWD Pages 4 & 5, Oct. 31, and Page 6, Nov. 7.)

Now WWD talks to the fashion pros in Paris, London, Washington, Boston, Chicago, Denver, Los Angeles and San Francisco to find out what they're thinking about The Lowdown.

IN PARIS

THE COUTURE IS HOT ON THE MIDI BUT TURNED OFF BY THE MAXI.

And when the maxi shows up on Paris streets it's usually on American girls or girls who've picked it up in London.

St. Laurent, Bohan, Givenchy and Cardin all like the Lowdown, but only Givenchy did the below-the-ankle for day last season and he admits it's got draw-backs.

"It's very limited. It should be either for evening or for the country. In the city it looks like somebody's out in her dressing gown."

"It's for pop singers," says St. Laurent. "I like the midcalf length because it shows the best part of the leg and you can play with it. I certainly would never think of maxis for daytime."

"It's grotesque," says Bohan about the maxi. "Private clients who recently ordered day suits and coats in normal lengths are coming back to have their hemlines dropped to Midi length."

"It's absurd," says Cardin who defines maxi as reaching the floor. "My favorite length is above the ankle because it's pretty to see the slimmest part of the leg. The floor length? How can you expect a woman walking, climbing stairs, or driving her car with coats and dresses sweeping the floor?"

AND THE MIDI IS EITHER OUTSELLING EVERY-THING ELSE IN THESE FOUR HOUSES or it's the definite white hope of the vendeuses for the next season.

Givenchy reports 50 per cent of its sales in long lengths, of which four-fifths are maxi . . . mainly for evening.

At St. Laurent 40 per cent of the day clothes are Midi and 70 per cent of the evening clothes are below calf.

At Dior only 3 per cent of the sales are long, but Andree de Vilmorin says "it will be the big thing the winter after this."

At Cardin the long lengths account for about 5 per cent of the sales.

IN LONDON

THE LOWDOWN IS CALLED "ANKLE-LENGTH."

Designers have their own ideas on the Lowdown lengths.

"Both the Midi and the maxi are finished," says Ossie Clark. "The newest and the best length just shows the ankle."

"I like the long coat . . . to the ankle, very full and swirly," says Jean Muir. "It looks marvelous opened over pants and worn with boots."

"I'm bored with the Midi," says Barbara Hulanicki of Biba's.

"There's no use saying one is better than the other," says designer John Bates. "It depends who's wearing it and how it's put together. I like the Midi coat over a maxi skirt or pants, a maxi coat over a Midi skirt, or pants tucked into boots."

But those London birds know what they want. They're putting together the Lowdown lengths like the Midi coat over the maxi skirt or pants.

IN LOS ANGELES

IT'S THE ALL-WEATHER MAXI . . . in vinyl and can-vas.

Retailers also say the knit cardigan Midi over pants is a big seller.

"The Midi and maxi dress will only catch on with the woman who has a truly extensive wardrobe and wants to round it out with another look," says Amelia Gray, of Beverly Hills. "The longer lengths, particularly the Midi, have an aging effect on mature women. The young people can get away with long lengths and come out beautiful people."

"Both the Midi and the maxi have marvelous looks, but we have not committed ourselves in any depth on long dresses," says Norman Wechsler, vice-president, fashion merchandising, J. W. Robinson Co. "The longer lengths in cocktail dresses, however, will improve in sales in the next few months."

"Maxis are fashionable at the moment, but I don't think they'll have a long life," says Galanos. "I don't know which direction we will go for spring. The shorter skirt is contemporary, the other lengths are play act-ing. The maxi looks ridiculous on the street. For day the look should be short."

IN BOSTON

RETAILERS ARE CALLING THE MAXI THE "OUT-ERWEAR WINNER OF THE YEAR."

And it's the young who are the biggest maxi fans

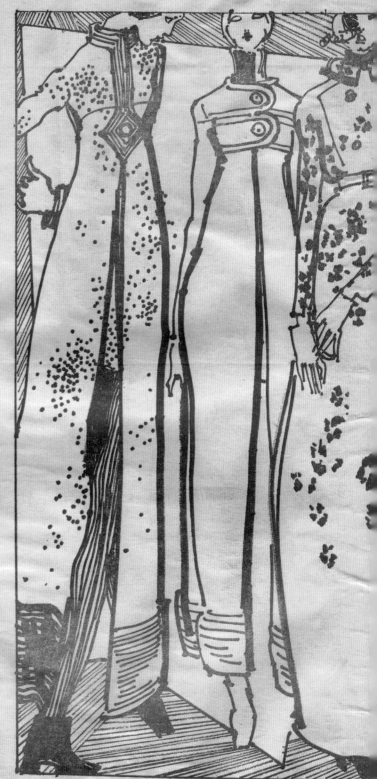

THE PARIS COUTURE BEST SELLERS.

CARDIN'S MAXI COAT . . . in green and white tweed with green vinyl rolls at hemline, neck-line and cuffs worn over matching mini skirt.

CARDIN'S RUST WOOL MAXI COAT . . . over black turtle-neck and mini skirt also in rust wool.

GIVENCHY'S M RAINCOAT . printed panther.

... even "young marrieds in their 30s and a few older women." They also say that sales of maxi coats didn't decrease after the initial college selling period ended.

The Midi is almost a nonentity in Boston. Several stores are carrying them in dresses, suits and coats with pants ensembles, but most retailers report they are "moving a lot slower than the maxi . . . there's little call for them."

"We're reordering as many maxis as we can," says Andrew D. Hooker, managing director Lord & Taylor. "We feature the Midi more quietly and elegantly, but there isn't much call for it here."

"We're carrying both lengths," says Robert Hoye, executive vice-president, Jordan Marsh. "The maxi's selling better."

"We have a few Midi pieces, but there isn't much call for that length," says Robert Banks, Jr., general manager, Bonwit Teller.

"Maxi coats have been very big with junior customers and teen customers, particularly in rainwear. We expect the mid-length to take over, but we have little sign of it now," says Richard Shapiro, Filene's chairman.

IN WASHINGTON

THE MAXI IS THE STRONGER SELLER BY FAR . . . partly because most stores have stocked very few Midis.

Maxi selling has been strongest in junior and young departments and moderate price ranges. Initially maxi raincoats in canvas and vinyl were the most popular, now it's the untrimmed wool maxi.

"The maxi has sold very well," says Tom Parker, vice-president and rtw general merchandise manager, Woodward & Lothrop. "We haven't had too many Midis in store. It has been very limited in the market."

"The maxi is a multi-purpose coat," says Gerry Solovei, designer coat and suit buyer, Julius Garfinckel, "the Midi isn't. It can't be worn for evening or over pants . . . and look right both ways."

"For us, maxi sales have increased since college business," says Hank Hemsing, divisional merchandise manager, The Hecht Co. "It started in junior rainwear and has moved into other areas."

IN SAN FRANCISCO

THE MAXI COAT IS MAKING THE STRONG MARK ON SALES FIGURES.

And maxi sales have not dropped since the college rush. Instead coat departments are reporting steadily increasing figures.

Retailers believe the more the maxi is seen on the street the more popular it becomes. And this fact, plus cold San Francisco weather makes them expect even better sales.

Midi pants and dresses are only items. Most stores bought only a few to feature in window displays and have found the demand does not show any need for more.

Joseph Magnin is the biggest seller of the Lowdown lengths. They report the canvas all-weather maxi at about $40 to be one of their best sellers.

IN CHICAGO

THE MAXI IS THE BIG COVER UP NEWS.

Even after college opened, maxi coats sold stronger than ever.

Store reactions to the Midi length vary . . . "the Midi length is a bomb," "the girls hate the length" and "Midis sold only with pants." Some say, however, "Midi business is quite good, but the maxi is best. And not just to the young kids."

The maxi is selling best in coats, especially for day and under $100.

Marshall Field's reports that both their jersey and argyle maxis from Jill Jrs. in the Young Chicago Coat and Suit area are "selling extremely well." Bramson's best selling maxi is Outer, Ltd.'s double-breasted navy blue coat. And at John T. Shayne's it's Giardi's double-breasted slightly flared maxi.

IN DENVER

THE MAXI IS ALSO THE BIG WINNER.

There are few or no Midis stocked in department stores and no requests for them. But buyers say they plan to bring a few Midis in for spring to see how they'll go.

William Neustéter, associated buyer of moderate price coats at Neusteter's: "We haven't brought any Midis into the department, but we've placed some spring orders for December delivery. We are still getting good reaction to our maxis."

James Slayden, general merchandise manager of May-D&F: "We do not have any Midis in stock but we'll have a few in for spring."

Jan Johnston, coat buyer at Fashion Bar: "We had some Midis earlier, but customers went for the sweeper length for fall. We've had no requests for Midis and we're holding off for spring until we see the total market."

NCHY'S MIDI . . . in black sashed at the

GIVENCHY'S MIDI EVENING DRESS . . . in black crepe belted at the waist.

ST. LAURENT'S MIDI COAT . . . in Racine jersey over tunic and pants.

ST. LAURENT'S MIDI SUIT . . . the short blouson jacket and wrap skirt in brown and white tweed.

Drawing by Kenneth Paul Block

In 1969, Kenneth Paul Block (Kenneth) documented the "longuette" hemline controversy. Given his long tenure at *WWD*, it is interesting to compare Kenneth's drawing style at different points in time. In his work at the end of the sixties, the use of graphics gives the newly elongated figures a sense of place. Charcoal pencil has been exchanged for a felt-tip pen, perhaps to accommodate changes in graphic reproduction technologies. A partial rendering conveys the sixties' preference for textures and patterns.

Steven Stipelman repeated a pleasing layout in these two illustrations featured in *WWD* on November 12, 1969. By overlapping each figure, Stipelman created the illusion of depth within the picture plane. As in all fashion art, garment details are prioritized in the hierarchy of imagery.

One of the Fairchild Business Newspapers

Women's Wear Daily

THE RETAILER'S DAILY NEWSPAPER ®

Vol. 117 No. 49 ★ ★   NEW YORK, N. Y., MONDAY, SEPTEMBER 9, 1968   TEN CENTS   One Year $24 Payable in Advance

Tito Forces On Alert, He Raps Reds

By MICHAEL GUNTON
Cable Fairchild News Service®

BELGRADE, Yugoslavia. — Marshal Tito is quietly mobilizing units of the Yugoslavian Army, heavy military activity is reported on the Rumanian frontier while units of the Yugoslavian Air Force are being deployed around major airfields including Belgrade and Zagreb.

Meanwhile Marshal Tito continued his verbal attacks on the Russians Friday, denouncing their invasion of Czechoslovakia and calling for immediate withdrawal of all Warsaw Pact troops.

While military activity and indignant posture may

See TITO'S, Page 29

Czech Crisis: Winter Follows Springtime

By G. Y. DRYANSKY
Cable Fairchild News Service®

(The writer of this article just returned from Czechoslovakia where he covered the Russian occupation.)

PARIS. — There were posters and slogans in Russian and Czech on every wall and store window, like a rash that was a critical point of some disease from which the city suffered.

I'd come too late for Dubcek's euphoric "springtime," as the Czechs called their nine months of ideo-

See CZECH, Page 29

Red Smith, America's leading sportswriter, now appears daily in WWD. His column today is on Page 14.

THE BLACK MARKET

Drawing by Richard Thornton

Fairchild News Service®

NEW YORK.—The Negro consumer is being given the hard sell in 1968 and it's no wonder.

His income is rising and the color of his money would make any businessman smile.

Somewhat overlooked in the millions

Continued on Page 4

Tiny Fur Shops Face The Knife

By SANDY PARKER

NEW YORK. — The fur industry is approaching a juncture which could well determine the fate of many small firms and the course of the industry itself. The question is how long the industry can continue consisting of tiny shops?

The fur union, preparing to negotiate a new contract by Feb. 15, thinks the undercapitalized manufacturer with the three-man factory is an anachronism in view of the ever-increasing needs of the worker.

Declares Furriers Joint Council manager George Stofsky: "The fur worker has as much right to expect security in his industry as another worker gets

See SMALLER, Page 29

Moscow goes Bourgeois

Fairchild News Service®

MOSCOW.—The Intourist guide was not wearing one of her mini-skirts, even though the head office had ordered it for "fashion-minded" visitors. At least she didn't consider it a mini-skirt, although it was enough centimeters above the knee to count as indecent Western fashion in some other countries.

There was champagne with huge fresh strawberries along with the home-cooked lunch at a professor's home up near Moscow University in the Lenin Hills. It was hard

Continued on Page 20

Russ Togs Is Afire for Acquisitions

NEW YORK. — The collapse of merger talks between Russ Togs, Inc. and American Tobacco Co. has apparently soured Russ Togs president Eli L. Russo on the idea of merging with a larger company.

"I'm not particularly ready to merge with anyone. If someone wants to merge with us, they'll have to come and look for us, we're not going to look for them," Russo told WWD.

Russo instead plans to turn his attention toward expansion of his company through acquisitions. What

See RUSS, Page 17

FOCUS

Meyer Gets Ready To Spread Wings

NORWICH, Conn. — John Meyer, president of the sportswear house bearing his name, has his eye on $100 million volume and he plans to achieve this without pushing.

He has a formula to achieve this annual volume "in 10 years or less," and in a large part Meyer is relying on the growth of the nation.

But Meyer is taking steps to make his company grow along with the economy. The company, which will run up sales totaling about $30 million this year, is planning to open a junior division, which Meyer figures will add at least $5 million in the first year, and $10 million the second.

John Meyer of Norwich had total sales of $26 million last year, and $20 million in 1966.

All this growth and expansion could suggest a merger or public offering for the now privately-held company, but Meyer discounts this.

"We like our independence. Either a merger or public offering would cause us to lose some of it," Meyer explains. "At the present time we like our private (cor-

See MEYER, Page 30

The Polls Agree

NOTES

1. *Quotations from Mao Zedong,* published in 1967 came to be popularly known as the Little Red Book.

2. Robert Storr, *Gerhard Richter October 18, 1977* (New York: The Museum of Modern Art, 2000), pp. 82–83.

4. Thomas Hine, *Populuxe* (New York: Alfred A. Knopf, 1986), p. 3.

5. Jonathan M. Woodham, *Twentieth Century Ornament* (Rizzoli International Publications, 1990).

6. Refers to the DuPont slogan coined in 1935 celebrating science as savior. Available at: www.Delawareonline.com (Maureen Milford, staff reporter, business news, June 30, 2002).

7. Timothy Leary, Ralph Metzner, and Richard Alpert, *The Psychedelic Experience: A Manual Based on The Tibetan Book of The Dead* (Citadel Press, 1976).

8. Jesse Kornbluth, *Pre-Pop Warhol* (New York: Random House, 1988).

9. H. H. Arnason, *History of Modern Art* (Englewood Cliffs, N.J.: Prentice-Hall and Harry N. Abrams, 1977), p. 625. Out of print.

10. Charlotte Seeling, *Fashion: The Century of the Designer, 1900–1999* (Konemann Verlagsgesellschaft), p. 362.

11. Richard Martin and Harold Koda, *Haute Couture* (New York: The Metropolitan Museum of Art, 1995), p. 35. Distributed by Harry N. Abrams.

12. Jone Johson Lewis, www.womenhistory.about.com.

13. Seeling, *Fashion: The Century of the Designer*, p. 362.

14. In an interview with the author, Robert Passantino referred to this negative space as the "hell shape."

15. Interview with Linda Angrilli in *FIT Network* 12, no. 4 (2002).

16. William Claxton and Peggy Moffitt, *The Rudi Gernreich Book* (New York: Rizzoli International Publications, 1991).

17. Mablen Jones, *Getting It On, The Clothing of Rock and Roll* (Abbeville Press, 1987).

WWD70s

"...I think the more women demand liberty, the more they lose it."

Coco Chanel (1970)

The youth cult's opposition to traditional values in the sixties opened the door to a social free-for-all in the following decade. Preoccupation with psychedelic drug use, free love, and Eastern philosophy served to divert the "me" generation from the tall task at hand: replacing the objectionable institutions and standards torn down in their rebellion.[1]

Fewer restrictions and broad experimentation fostered an atmosphere of chaotic freedom. Second-wave baby boomers came of age ahead of schedule when eighteen-year-olds were granted the right to vote in 1972. With expanded career opportunities available to them, women entered the workforce in greater numbers. Along with the hippie credo to "make love not war," the gay rights movement took on even greater momentum. The ecology movement, which began as part of the rebound from futurism, was kicked into high gear by the 1972 OPEC oil embargo. There was also a growing awareness of the heritage of the past prompting active support for the preservation of historic sites.

The hippie style lived on in the beginning of the seventies, with love beads, Roman sandals, and acid-color textiles inspired by flowers, butterflies, and art nouveau. The continuing "longuette" controversy in *WWD* was evidence of the free reign given to choices elsewhere in society. With the old rules and fashion dictates gone, the options available, such as the midi and hot pants, were extreme in scope. Flower Power was still in full swing, but by 1971, advocacy of the psychedelic experience was beginning to fade. The sixties' much-heralded combination of sex, drugs, and rock and roll extracted a heavy price as substance abuse claimed the lives of rock legends Janis Joplin, Jimi Hendrix, and Jim Morrison. The tensions of the times weighed heavily on the diminishing idealism of maturing baby boomers. Television documented the radical societal changes taking place in the face of outspoken resistance. The moral issues raised by conscientious objection to the war in Vietnam rendered gray areas of lawful behavior and patriotic duty.

Student protests continued to challenge the American status quo. The Nixon administration's 1970 invasion of Cambodia and the influence of covert government intelligence on national policy raised the ante for political dissent. Back in 1968, antiwar protestors led by the Chicago Seven at the Republican National convention were provoked by the aggressive actions of Mayor Daly's police force and then assailed as rioters. After armed confrontation at Kent State University in Ohio left four people dead in 1970, protestors began to realize that more than ideology was at stake; political activism had become a life-threatening proposition.

The jubilation of newly emancipated 18-year-olds was dampened by the reelection of Richard

M. Nixon that same year. Not long after, scandalous revelations by an anonymous source known as Deep Throat prompted a full Senate investigation of Nixon's "dirty tricks" in the 1972 presidential campaign. The Watergate hearings and impending impeachment ultimately forced President Nixon to resign from office.

As in the sixties, seventies' street life was transformed into aesthetics, with the student revolt influencing fashion. Flower Power dressing had been a political statement from the start. Saint Laurent, who had participated in the French student demonstrations, drew inspiration from the sweaters and jeans that had become the uniform of international student protest. *WWD* declared 1973 the "year of the sweater," and knitwear became a popular antifashion statement. Sweater dressing gradually evolved to more sophisticated looks, such as Halston's tubular knits and Chanel's knitted suits. In 1974, Diane von Furstenberg used bold prints on stretchy new

synthetics to create her classic soft wrap dress. The sexual freedom of the hippie culture was expressed in fashion with provocative sheer blouses, body stockings, hot pants, cropped tops, and hip hugger pants.

The ideas as well as the affectations of the hippie culture were gradually absorbed into the mainstream. Antiwar sentiment spread and mass protests took place as once-upright citizens flaunted their disregard for untenable laws by smoking marijuana and dodging the draft. Renegade behavior extended beyond the bohemian fringe and was reflected in the popular culture. In the late sixties, Jacqueline Susann's thinly veiled fiction novel about the downward spiral of three ambitious women into the *Valley of the Dolls* was an indictment of epidemic prescription drug abuse in the middle class. Banking on the success of *Bonnie and Clyde*, Hollywood continued to celebrate the antihero in films such as *The Godfather* (1972) and *Taxi Driver* (1976). Anti-heroes inspired anti-fashion, and gangster suits for men and women became a popular extension of the sixties' unisex trend.

Years of struggle about issues of race, gender, and foreign policy had left the baby boom generation unable to reconcile the disparity between expectation and reality. Mistrust of government, vague social mores, and the first economic decline since World War II were more than enough to shock a generational psyche already made fragile by the events of the sixties. A major shift in attitude occurred as the passionate belief in a better future was replaced by introspection and cynicism. Members of the newly labeled "me" generation were hooked on retro and the diversion of a romanticized past. Nostalgia matured and intensified throughout the decade as loose interpretations of the past became the foundation for the postmodernism of the eighties.

As the shell-shocked baby boomers matured, seventies' designers began looking beyond customary sources of inspiration for age-appropriate fashion. The sixties' invention of the microchip contradicted the idea of form following function. The minimalist aesthetic, first espoused by the Bauhaus in 1919, had run its course. The combination of expanded consciousness and exposure to exotic cultures led designers down an entirely new path. Lush, abundant, cluttered looks appeared in all of the applied arts.[2] Victoriana, art nouveau, orientalism, and art deco were referenced as textures and patterns in the new thriftshop chic. Revisitation of the arts and crafts movement created a trend for hand knits, macramé, and crochet. Handmade, one-of-a-kind, ethnic looks, such as batiks and tie-dyes, were eventually appropriated for the mass market by machine production.

Societal issues that initially precipitated these historic art movements were also revisited. Like the Victorian era, the seventies was a period of new invention and social responsibility. Just as the Victorians' decorative formulas had been

LEFT: Eiri, Japanese erotica (shunga). Courtesy, Stuart Jackson Gallery. Reprinted with permission.

RIGHT: Michelangelo, (1475–1564). *Leda and the Swan*. Courtesy, © The National Gallery, London.

a rejection of the industrial revolution, the psychedelic imagery of the seventies reflected a spurning of technology. The sixties' blurring of major and minor arts paralleled the art nouveau preference for handmade objects in the face of industrialization.

The renewed focus on Japonisme and orientalism was a throwback to art nouveau, but also a reflection of the seventies' new East-West diplomacy. In 1972, the United States' acceptance of the People's Republic of China and Taiwan as the "two Chinas" was the first step in normalizing dipomatic relations with the communist superpowers. Intent on bolstering his approval rating in a reelection year, President Nixon set off on

groundbreaking trips to Moscow and Beijing. The appearance of chinoiserie and cossack looks in fashion had a direct correspondence to Nixon's trips.

The influence of the Japanese was also paramount in seventies' design innovation. In the years following World War II, there was a strong negative reaction against their own industrial practices, which many associated with the war effort. Young Japanese designers began traveling to other parts of the world to experience new design ideas and industrial technologies firsthand. The Osaka World's Fair Exposition in 1970 brought reciprocal international attention to traditional Japanese design. As Japan grew to become a leading economic power, the West looked to the East for product and design innovations. Moreover, products stamped "made in Japan" were no longer thought of as disposable junk. Building on accumulated successes, young Japanese designers confidently asserted their new, technology-influenced aesthetic. The Japanese fashion designers Rei Kawakubo, Kenzo Takada, Issey Miyake, Hanae Mori, and Yohji Yamamoto were schooled and apprenticed in Paris. But owing to the Japanese tradition of prioritizing textile and drape, their collections were radically different from all couture and ready-to-wear that came before.[3]

Influences from the Pacific Rim were incorporated into the larger seventies' trend of multiculturalism. Triggered, in part, by the hippies' exploration of alternative lifestyles and philosophies, anything perceived to be exotic had new appeal. The civil rights movement and increasing media coverage of world affairs in the sixties also contributed to the emphasis on cultural diversity. Pop diva Cher buoyed her celebrity status by playing up her Native-American heritage. In 1971, the film *Shaft*, with a musical score by Isaac Hayes, was the first African-American action film. Subsequent action, sci-fi, horror, and western films featured all-black casts and production crews. The eighties' hip-hop movement would be cultural heir to the seventies "blaxploitation" film genre.

JAPANESE STYLE

Multiculturalism was pivotal to the changing aesthetic of the seventies. Traditions and cultures of the world were assimilated into fashion design in feminine, voluminous peasant looks made from natural fibers. Saint Laurent was inspired by new global sources for gypsy, cossack, and gaucho looks. Bold, graphic textiles from Marimekko, the Finnish industrial collective, were popular for apparel, accessories, and interior design. Department stores such as Henri Bendel, Bloomingdale's, and Bergdorf Goodman began to offer exotic merchandise in bazaarlike retail environments. By the end of the seventies, silhouettes inspired by North African caftans, Tibetan robes, Indian saris, and Japanese kimonos concealed and swathed the body. "At-home" clothes and loungewear were especially influenced by the eastern design aesthetic. New garment shapes had less and less to do with human anatomy and, often, were "one size fits all." Silhouettes that previously hugged the body took on increased volume and drape by the end of the decade.

Standards of beauty were reconsidered in light of the new multiculturalism. A preference for exotic looks created new opportunities for models of all racial backgrounds. Much to their chagrin, sixties' nymphets were maturing in the seventies. The fixation with maintaining a youthful appearance helped make fitness a national pastime for both men and women. The "natural look" was preferred, although not easily achieved. Sporty, active looks were contrived by artificially highlighting hair and maintaining year-round chemical tans. The popularity of the Afro hairstyle in the African-American community inspired Caucasian men and women to process their hair with permanent waves. Cosmetics and hair care became a thriving industry, so much so that the film *Shampoo* satirized the idea of hairdresser as guru.

The influence of multiculturalism began to be

seen in other aspects of the popular culture, as well. By the late sixties, disco—a fusion of Latin rhythms and electronically synthesized music—became popular in the gay community. A driving electronic beat was mixed from one song to the next to create a nonstop dance track. The discoteque eventually became an entertainment venue for the masses. As celebrated in the film *Saturday Night Fever*, the disco culture inspired body-conscious clothing for both men and women. Synthetic fibers provided low-maintenance luxury and softer drape in glamorous art deco silhouettes. Heat-transfer prints on Banlon and Qiana shirts and dresses were the costume of choice for disco's tightly choreographed dance.

The driving soundtrack that started the fad for disco was only one of many evolving categories in contemporary music. Album-oriented rock music became a big business and had increasing ties to fashion. Concerts took place in larger venues, moving from the intimacy of smoke-filled night-clubs to cavernous arenas. "Glamrock" antiheroes began to adopt an over-the-top flamboyant style for higher visibility in stadium performances. Early in the seventies, avant-garde rock groups such as the New York Dolls traded in their fashionable gangster suits for tongue-in-cheek androgynous dressing. Funk bands were particularly theatrical in their constant reinvention of outrageous personae and costumes for each tour. George Clinton renamed his Parliaments the Funkadelics, and sixties' tuxedos were replaced by far-out psychedelic costumes. As contemporary music performances became multimedia extravaganzas, rock stars began to enlist the services of fashion designers. In 1973, David Bowie, already famous for his "art rock" fashion sense, recruited Kansai Yamamoto to design his costumes in the spirit of traditional Japanese theater. The following year, Bowie left glamrock behind to become the thin white duke from outer space in the Nicolas Roeg film, *The Man Who Fell to Earth*.

Followers of rock style got a second chance to wear white suits in 1977, with the release of *Saturday Night Fever* and the culmination of disco culture at New York's Studio 54. The decade concluded with the apocalyptic street style of the first punk rock musicians.[4]

Earlier in the decade, Seventh Avenue fashion evolved in tandem with world and social events. Designers catered to newly empowered women asserting their individuality. Styles such as Halston's ultrasuede shirtdress were not restricted by age or profession, but rather a current trend subject to personal interpretation. In 1970, Saint Laurent designed safari pantsuits for both men and women. With social requirements for dress eliminated, the pantsuit was considered appropriate for office, school, and evenings out. Bellbottoms, knickers, hot pants, palazzos, and jumpsuits became popular alternatives for a woman's new active lifestyle. By 1973, haute couture was modernized to accommodate the revolution in fashion. Lenient new rules required fewer sample hands and reduced the number of garments required for collections. As a result, both couture and ready-to-wear were infused with new life by the arrival of young, avant-garde designers such as Thierry Mugler, Jean Paul-Gaultier, and Vivienne Westwood. Multimedia coverage of the collections caused runway shows to borrow heavily from interactive performance art and rock concerts, with both garments and presentation designed for the camera.

As in the sixties, there was a rebounding of opposing trends in a single decade. The seventies began with a rural arts and crafts sensibility and an affinity for natural and recycled materials. Neutral and faded color palettes gave products a homespun or worn appearance. The practice of marketing to baby boomers carried over from the sixties. Mass production made it possible to produce more apparel than people needed; consumers had to be coerced into buying in excess.[5] Fashion and celebrity became mass-market commodities, and garment design increasingly was driven by advertising. Licensed apparel, such as Calvin Klein and Fiorucci jeans, began to appear in the marketplace, anticipating the designer branding that would peak in the eighties.

As marketing and advertising began to dominate design, the counterculture was undermined by its appropriation for the masses. *WWD* reported that even the aging Duchess of Windsor was wearing hot pants. Change was in the wind, in the service of both aesthetic cycles and the redefinition of rebellion. The counterculture began to take on an edginess that made it less accessible to the general public. The devaluation of the dollar caused by the OPEC oil embargo in 1972, was followed by a recession shortly thereafter. The seventies' economic downturn shifted the cultural focus from rural to urban, and the punk and new wave movements made their first appearance. Dissonant music, graffiti, and a costume of fetish leather and torn T-shirts expressed the new aesthetic of outrage.

By the late seventies, the subversion of good taste by the "anti design" philosophy of the Memphis Group in Milan was another visual manifestation of this sentiment.[6] As part of a rebounding cycle, there was renewed interest in technology after exotic and hand-crafted merchandise was simulated by mass production. Proponents of ad hocism began using ready-made industrial materials for residential decoration. Personal electronics, such as the answering machine and the Sony Walkman, came into common use. In 1977, Apple's introduction of the first fully assembled personal computer for consumers marked the beginning of the cyberculture.

Reflecting the seventies as a time of change, the *WWD* illustrations from this period document the escapism favored by a society in transition. Artists trafficked between real and unreal by flouting the rules of perspective in illogical compositions. A

Egon Schiele, *Female Nude.*
Courtesy, © Albertina
Museum. Reprinted with
permission.

carryover from the sixties, had opaque meaning and confusing messages. As art deco began to influence fashion, the *WWD* illustrations became austere studies of glamorous scenarios. Stylized figures were posed in unexpected ways with an impossible resemblance to human beings. Faces that defied stereotype were representative of a more individual standard of beauty. The seventies' multiculturalism was reflected in the racial diversity of both the fashion figures and the art staff at *WWD*.

The sixties' habit of referencing fine art and literature continued in the correspondence between illustration styles and the rapid series of trends in fashion. Art nouveau, Russian constructivism, expressionism, and art deco all were reflected in the illustrations: Catherine Clayton Purnell's decorative idiom is in the tradition of Alphonse Mucha; Joel Resnicoff directly referenced the film poster *Six Girls Seeking Shelter* by Vladimir and Georgii Stenberg; Glen Tunstull's halftone images

more decorative focus was inspired by art nouveau. Send-ups of an absurd reverence for fashion were an extension of the popular antiestablishment philosophy. Hypnotic psychedelia, a

are an homage to Egon Schiele; Pedro Barrios's
elongated forms owe a debt to Amedeo Modigliani
and oceanic art. Most significant is the recalling
of methods used by Georges Barbier, Edouardo
Garcia Benito, and Léon Bakst to illustrate fashion in *La Gazette du Bon Ton* from 1912 to 1925.
Such traditions were merely points of departure
for the *WWD* artists. Graphics, rather than literal
imagery, became the backbone of layouts.
Merchandise was still cleanly delineated, but in
a new context. Photographic conventions, such
as double exposure, sequential imaging, and
distortion, were imitated in the illustrations and
used to good effect.

Nineteen seventy-one saw the advent of two-
and four-color reproduction at *WWD*. In April
1972, Fairchild also began publishing *W*, a synop-
sis of fashion news repositioned for a consumer
audience. The magazine's higher production
values and larger page size afforded additional
opportunities for spectacular full-color art. As

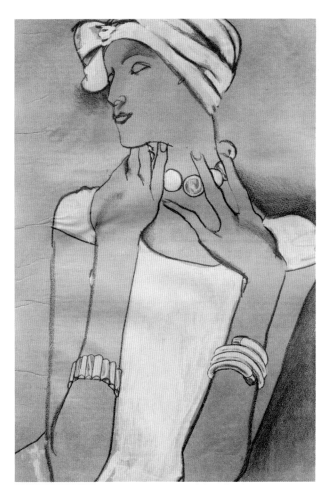

LE BASSIN D'ARGENT
Robe de diner garnie de ruban

Fevrier, 1920, Le Bassin D'Argent. *La Gazette Du Bon Ton.*

tively, with a flat application of paint within the lines of a contour drawing. Kenneth was accomplished in the technique of an academic watercolorist. His color is also flat, but passes beyond the contour of an object or shape. Kenneth's fluid use of transparent color accentuates the lines of a garment, blending so perfectly with the drawing that it is difficult to distinguish which came first. Broad, painterly brush strokes become graphic elements in the composition. In contrast, Stipelman's paintings rely on light and dark effects achieved by the spontaneous dabbing of opaque color. Line is secondary for Stipelman, part of his preliminary search for form. His compositions are defined by the impressionistic application of paint.[7]

journalists, the illustrators were compelled to accurately represent a garment's silhouette, surface, and color. But different methods and media served to distinguish each artist's individual approach. Passantino used color decora-

Many trends for women's wear were relevant to the children's market. Whimsical illustrations of children's fashions were regularly featured during the seventies. The appearance of children's drawings in *WWD* ended in 1985 when Fairchild began publishing *Children's Business*, a newspaper dedicated to the children's wear market.

The relaxed social climate and extensive creative license of this decade afforded the *WWD* illustrators an opportunity to tap their internal authority. Their visual language became more personal in the seventies and was not representative of any particular style or school of drawing. Applied formulas were rejected in favor of genuine sensitivity interpreted by good technique. During the seventies, *WWD* proved to be a wonderful showcase for the work of Analiese, Pedro Barrios, Kenneth Paul Block (Kenneth), Charles Boone, Stephen Cervantes, Deborah Marquit, Steven Meisel, Robert Melendez, Robert Passantino, Catherine Clayton Purnell, Joel Resnicoff, Steven Stipelman, and Glen Tunstull. Manufacturers sought them out to illustrate merchandise so that their advertisements in *WWD* would take on the appearance of editorial content. In comparison to their in-house work, these commissioned illustrations

Drawings by STEVEN MEISEL

seemed forced and self-conscious, constrained by the need to flatter the merchandise and please the client.[8]

By the end of the decade, a reaction against the prettiness of the revisited art movements contributed to the innovation of punk. As a newly hired illustrator, Meisel initially emulated the more senior artists. Imitation eventually gave way to a personal style that was an expression of his snarling punk sensibilities. The emergence of apoc-alyptic street fashion was illustrated according to a skewed, antidesign, "new wave" point of view. Like Antonio before him, Meisel would become a tastemaker. In swapping his pen for a camera, he would go on to superstardom in the eighties.

LONGUETTE POWER

Garment proportion was reconsidered in the seventies, with tiny tops and elongated bottoms.

Body-conscious clothing that exposed the midriff initiated fanatical fitness routines among the fashion forward. The western tradition of body-revealing silhouettes would change by the end of the decade as influential Japanese designers began emphasizing textile and drape in voluminous garments.

Robert Melendez's sporadic contribution to *WWD* spanned a period of three decades. After a successful stint as a member of the *WWD* art staff in the seventies, he dedicated his time to illustrating men's fashion at the *Daily News Record* (*DNR*). Melendez's work would occasionally appear in *WWD* in the eighties and more often in the nineties when he was commissioned as a freelancer.

THE YEAR OF

HE BUTTERFLY

After many seasons of coordinated separates, 1970 brought longer peasant and shirtwaist dresses that suited the bohemian mood. Millinery was an integral part of the granny look.

Robert Passantino's work is informed by a firsthand knowledge of children. Loving observations of his daughter Liza were incorporated into all of his drawings of children. The coded inclusion of Liza's name provided her with a visual treasure hunt. Well-placed geometric shadows give this otherwise flat composition a sense of depth, and an economy of line is used to indicate patterns and folds.

UP &

Stephen Cervantes's illustrations demonstrate the popularity of very long and very short clothing for both women and children. His artful compositions feature fine line work and flat washes reminiscent of the art deco style. Without any actual indication of a background, the children are posed to suggest a crowded sense of place. The women share equally tight quarters, and the size and arrangement of the figures creates an illusion of depth.

down

separate but together

Without exception, hot pants were mandatory for fashion followers in the seventies.

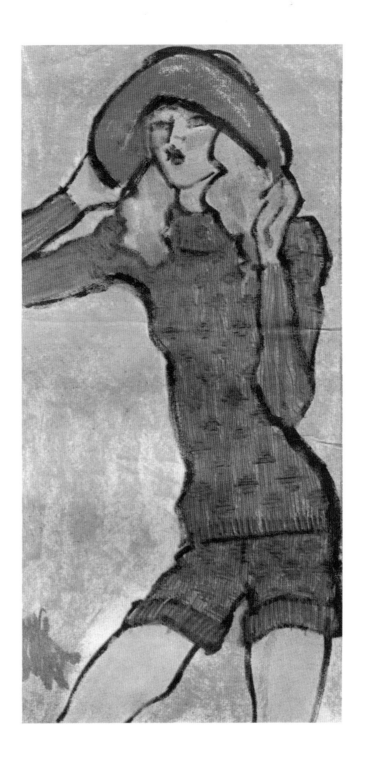

Kenneth Paul Block's (Kenneth) skill as an accomplished watercolorist is apparent in this early full-color illustration. The Banlon rib-knit sweater with matching hot pants was the height of fashion in 1971.

As seen in these illustrations by Kenneth Paul Block (Kenneth) (*this page*) and Pedro Barrios (*opposite*), the short over long fashion proportion had application for both womens wear and children's wear. Barrios's vivid imagination is seen in this illustration, which draws inspiration from Japanese woodcuts.

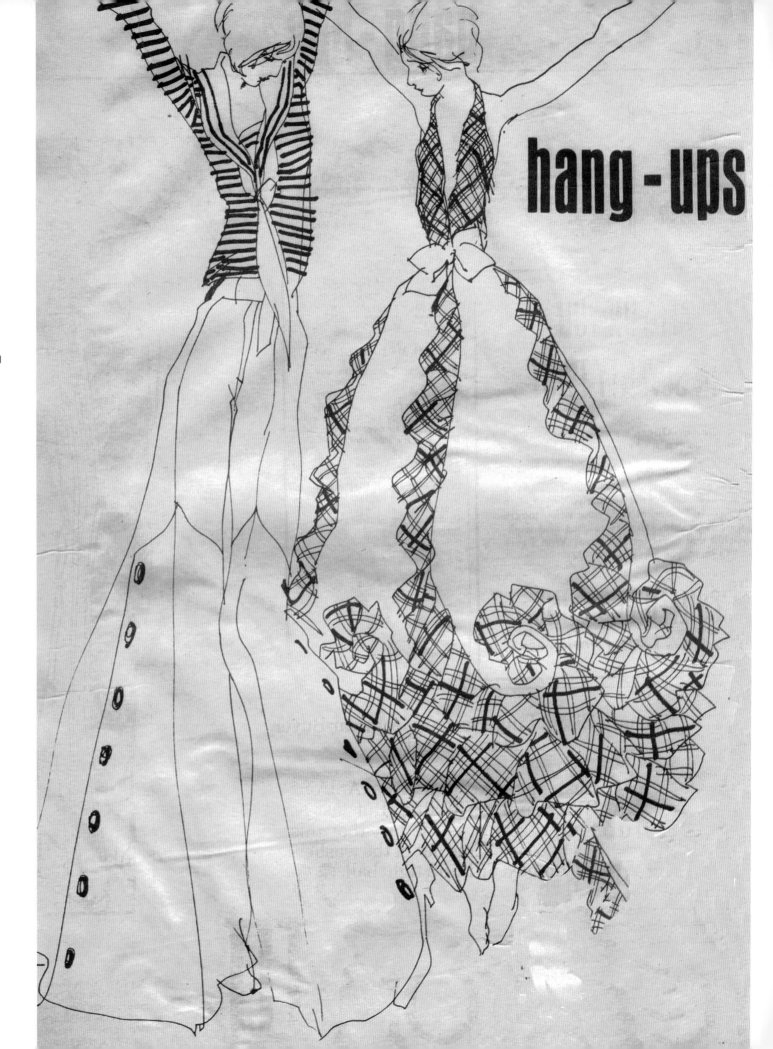

hang-ups

BARE BACK

Drawing by Robert Melendez

In continuation of the trend from the sixties, word art was used in surface designs for hosiery and apparel.

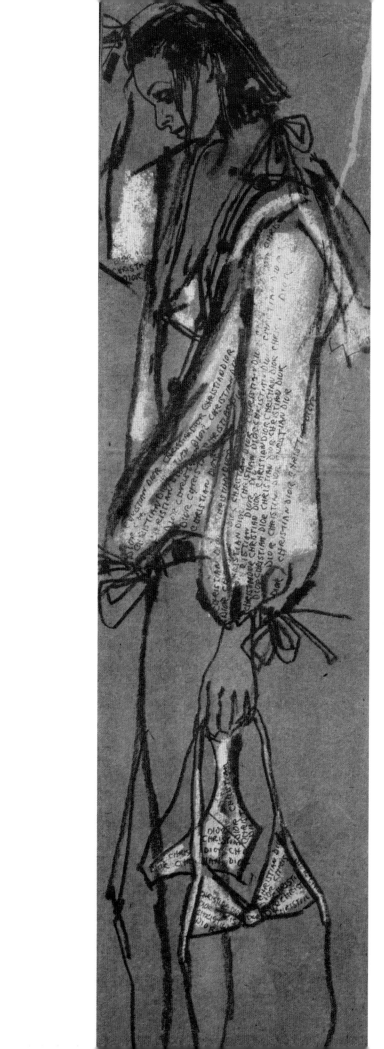

1673

Nineteen seventy-three was declared the "year of the knit" by *WWD*. Seventh Avenue designers such as Betsey Johnson, Liz Claiborne, and Stephen Burrows began designing knitted suits and separates in response to the international fashion trend.

Pedro Barrios's work reliably features more than a little mischief. In this illustration of sweater chic adapted from the uniform of student protest, he explored the possibilities of subversion and experimentation. His anatomically correct representation of the children pushes the boundaries of discretion.

NEEDLE-ING

Glen Tunstull's free application of wash is a more literal interpretation of surface interest. He sidestepped the risk of overworking this drawing with a skillful partial rendering. It is interesting to note that, in a pinch, Tunstull would draft Stephen Cervantes to model a daunting garment or assume a difficult pose.

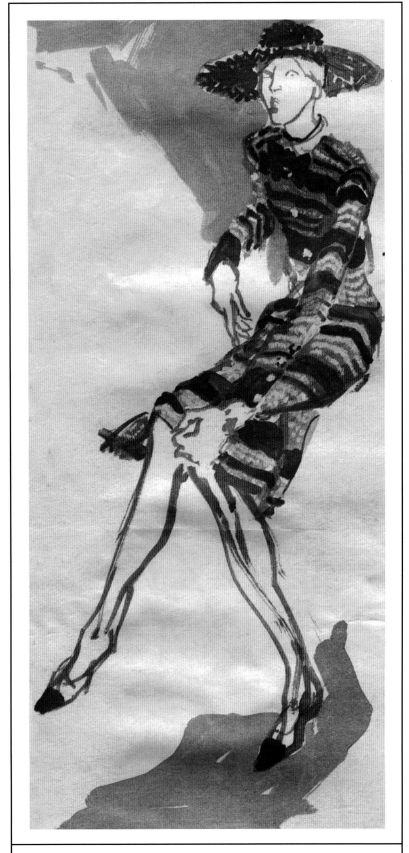

CHANEL ADVANCE

Dating back to 1926 when she designed the "little black dress," Chanel had always been a proponent of sweater dressing.

The popularity of chinoiserie in the early seventies was in direct correspondence to the new multiculturalism and diplomatic relations between the United States and The People's Republic of China.

The Chinese are here

These early examples of Robert Passantino's work capture the ornate sensibilities of the seventies. Passantino was hired right out of art school on the recommendation of Steven Stipelman. Passantino mastered his craft on the job and acted as a chameleon constantly reinventing himself throughout his career at *WWD*. With each new drawing style, Passantino built upon and disavowed an earlier approach.

During the seventies, personal electronics were developed for mainstream use. Intel had been formed in 1968, and by 1971, the first commercial microprocessors were introduced in the marketplace. Consumers began to favor electronics over mechanical devices, heralding the transition to a cyberculture.

taking
the
plunge

free
form

Robert Melendez's surreal composition relies on an ambiguous orientation and plays with the concept of three dimensional space. Multicultural sophisticates were the exotic inspiration for fashion and art. In this drawing, the precision of the delicate penwork and flat application of washes is consistent with the decorative style popular during the seventies.

NEW YORK —

    Lacy bodyshirts are the Civilized tops, feminine, demure over pantyhose that tip the legs with matching color.

    Danskin's waxes romantic in the Victorian mood, smocking and ruffles on high neck and cuffs. Sarah Melvin does it in embossed-like lace, color-teams it with quasi opaque pantyhose in white, black, beetroot, chianti and purple (left).

    Roman Stripe's goes lacy in floral pattern. Maria Marzan streamlines it with tiny stand-up collar, matches it up with Agilon opaque pantyhose in crimson, inky violet, wine, black, brown and navy (right).

Robert Passantino's signature use of mirrored images imitates his own personal life, as he is one of twin brothers.

In this illustration, Pedro Barrios reinterpreted Victoriana through a pop art lens. By juxtaposing the cosmic and the mundane, Barrios created a magical reality not unlike the visuals featured on the BBC TV show *Monty Python's Flying Circus*.

Thriftshop chic was an important facet of the seventies' preoccupation with the "good old days." Barrios's delineation of the camisole and knickers displays a romantic ephemera with a delicate eroticism that also recalls the Victorian past.

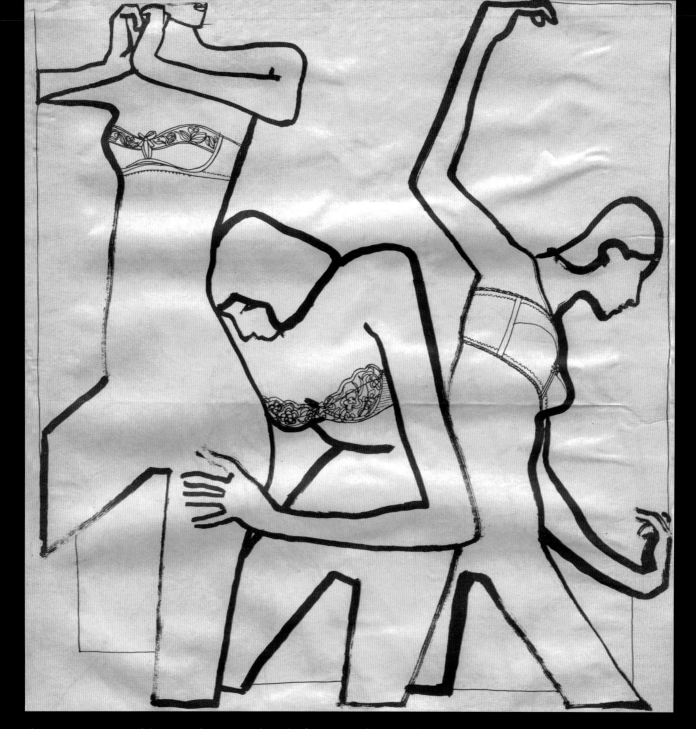

The *WWD* illustrations were not subject to the same level of censorship as photography. These seductive tableaus antici- pate postfeminism and the ironic sexual objectification of women. The powerful black outline in this illustration recalls the cubist

forms of Fernand Leger. Garment details are prioritized by the elimination of extraneous detail. The circumstance of the figures adds human interest without detracting from the merchandise.

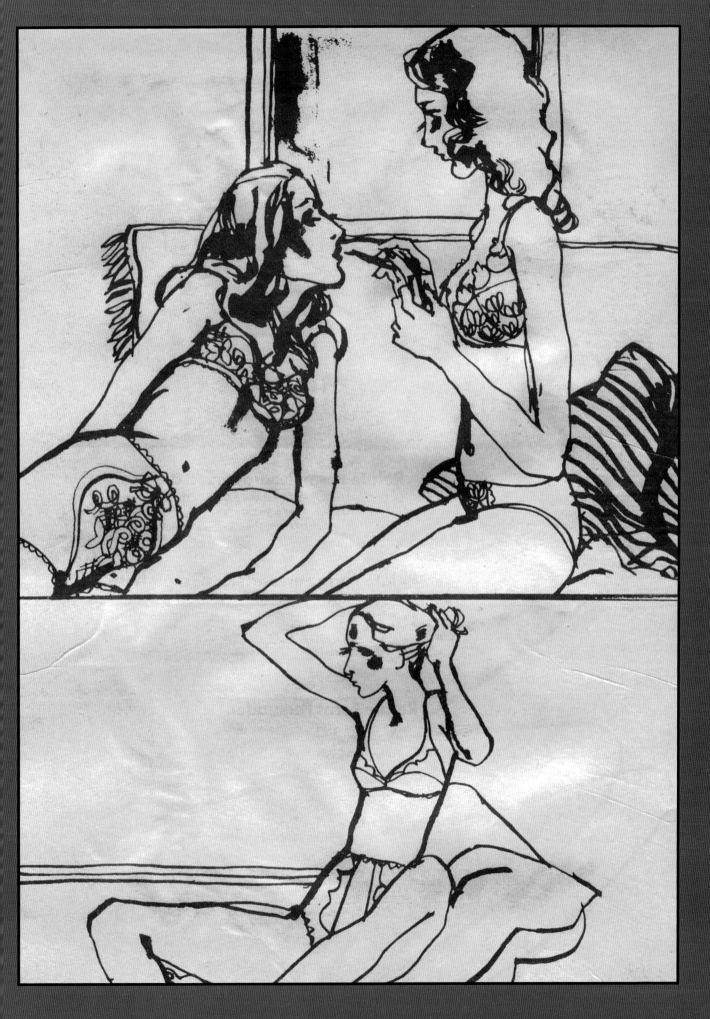

The narrative content of this layout reflects an elegant and decadent lifestyle with implied homoerotic experimentation. The viewer is introduced to the merchandise as an unwitting voyeur.

A camouflage pattern is used in this illustration by Robert Melendez as a textile motif and also suggests a landscape. The artful manipulation of scale and pattern is a carryover from sixties' experimentation with surrealism and collage. Synthesizing earlier pop art sensibilities and the seventies' decorative spirit, *WWD* illustrators began to use pressure-sensitive graphics in their work. Rub-off transfer sheets and patterned film originally were developed as a way of simulating continuous tone in line art. The preference for ornament led manufacturers such as Chartpak, Zipatone, and Letraset to add a wide variety of patterns and textures to their catalogs.

In this illustration by Analiese, surplus film that is a remnant of negative space is incorporated as a design element.

The relationship between film and fashion intensified during the seventies. The release of *The Godfather* in 1972 inspired tuxedo and gangster pantsuits for women and children. The costumes for *Annie Hall*, designed by Ralph Lauren, started a trend in women's wear for oversized mannish clothing. *Shaft* initiated a wave of funk fashion that eventually morphed into hip-hop. The nostalgic decadence of *Cabaret* and *The Night Porter* translated into S and M looks in makeup and photography. The cult following for *The Rocky Horror Picture Show* marked the arrival of punk, while *Alien* and *Star Wars* anticipated the high-tech trends of the eighties.

the goddaugter suit

TEA PARTY

Catherine Clayton Purnell's vivid imagination was shown to best advantage in children's wear illustrations. Her sumptuous compositions, which are romantic fantasies, set her apart from other *WWD* illustrators. Her work is less spontaneous, but far more narrative.

LIVING GLAMOROUSLY

As members of the youth cult matured, sophistication and glamour had new appeal. In 1972 the biopic *Lady Sings the Blues* starring Diana Ross chronicled the life of the great jazz performer Billy Holiday (*opposite*). The film featured both the costumes and consequences of the high life.

HOLIDAY GARDENIA

In these illustrations, photomontage is used for special effect with then-editor Jean Griffin as a model. Glen Tunstull used the seated pose (*this page*) and man's best friend (*opposite*) to suggest a sense of place, mood, and lifestyle.

Go Bulldogs Go

Photo by Nick Machalaba

Raoul Calabro's bulldog collection with model Cesar.

Drawing by Glen Tunstull

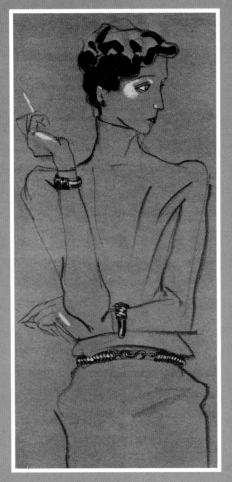

Glen Tunstull's signature use of toned paper began as an experiment in 1973. In this illustration, gray charcoal paper provides the background and mid-tones with dramatic black brush strokes defining shadows and mass. Light areas and highlights are achieved through the application of opaque white paint. Tunstull's use of poster white and toned paper was a throwback to fashion artist René R. Bouché and painter Egon Schiele. The disco culture also had an important influence on Tunstull's drawings of sophisticated women in glamorous situations.

MIX
MASTERS

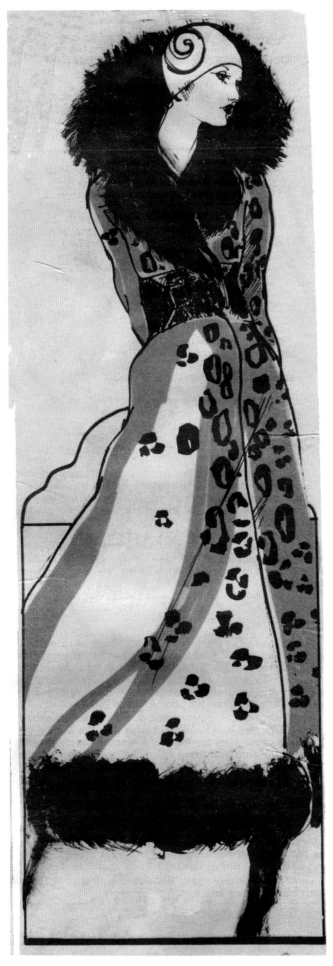

Before there was concern about the ethical treatment of animals, fur was a glamorous part of investment dressing. The fur business was revitalized in the seventies with silhouettes designed for a more youthful customer. Pelts were manipulated to the extreme with dyes, shearing, and stenciling, making them virtually unrecognizable from the source animal.

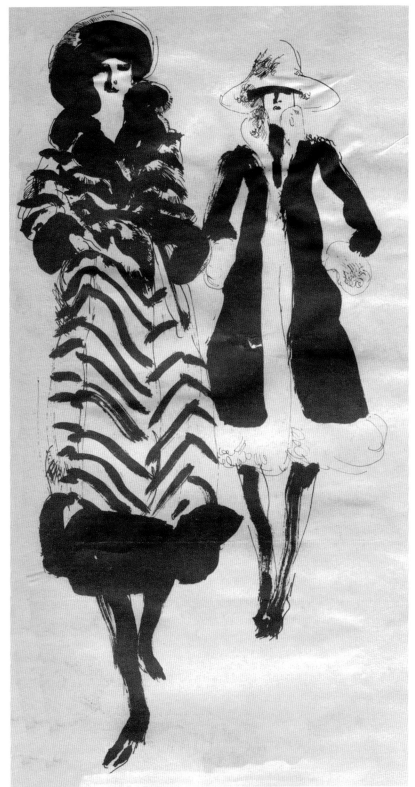

The skillful rendering of fur in these illustrations is accomplished through a combination of descriptive lines and washes that create the impression of lush softness and bulk. The partial rendering of the fur gives the drawings a varied and pleasing rhythm.

In this illustration, Pedro Barrios transferred his keen observations and multiple references to toned paper. (*Opposite*) The positioning of the hands and exaggerated proportion recall the work of Egon Schiele. Omission of the irises creates an ambiguity about the model's eyes and is reminiscent of an Amedeo Modigliani painting. The overall softness of the drawing corresponds to the textures of the angora headwrap and mohair sweater.

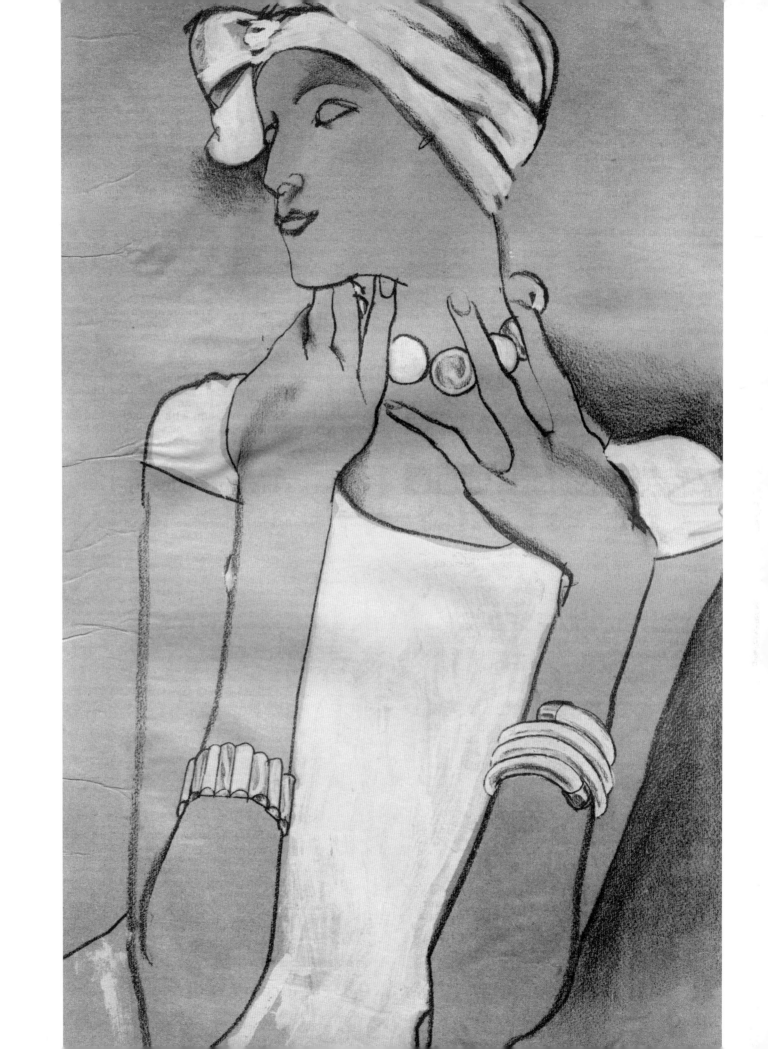

In 1975, Liberty of London celebrated its 100-year anniversary in a revival of the store's design archive. Printed cotton and wool challis were essential to the peasant and granny looks in seventies fashion.

In this drawing by Pedro Barrios, the enormity of the over-sized Afro is built upon the minutiae of tiny, repetitive pen strokes extending beyond the picture plane. The popularity of this African-American hairstyle prompted Caucasian men and women to style their hair with permanent waves.

Barrios's humor and style were always relative to the subject at hand. This composition illustrates a generic image announcing the debut of a Japanese line of skincare products. Using a minimum of efficient strokes, Barrios referenced Greek mythology (*Leda and the Swan*) for content and Japanese erotica (*shunga*) for style.

JAPANESE STYLE

In this illustration, Pedro Barrios's fashion figures sit atop bicycles, referencing the retro technology and travel imagery once popular in art deco style.

Achieved with either opaque or transparent media, Steven Stipelman's work became more painterly as his style evolved. The dresses in this illustration feature geometric embellishment that reflects art deco style.

COLOR IT SPRING

Stephen Cervantes's contour drawing does not rely on shadows and perspective to convey a sense of dimension. Volume is suggested by outline, and movement by curves. A crosshatch pattern defines the negative space and gives the seated figures a sense of place. The highly stylized faces bear an impossible resemblance to women and are a throwback to fashion illustrations first seen in *La Gazette du Bon Ton*.

Black shine

Nostalgia for art deco, a throwback to the glamour of the twenties, inspired both fashion and its representation in the seventies. Pedro Barrios's austere composition depends on strong black accents contrasting with finely drawn line work.

CROSSROADS

The deliberate simplicity of Stephen Cervantes's work paradoxically reveals a complete observation of form. Accommodating columns of text and advertising were perhaps the most inventive page designs featured in *WWD*.

Newsmakers

Joel Resnicoff's paper collage recalls the Stenberg brothers' poster for the film *Six Girls Seeking Shelter*. The figures in his amusing illustrations defy stereotype and are posed in unexpected ways. Inspired by observations of his mother and her friends, Resnicoff emphasized features that expressed individual character. He and Pedro Barrios both had an affinity for exaggeraed illustrations that bordered on caricature.

Fashion's inclination for social reversal is evident in Joel Resnicoff's illustration of a dishcloth dress and matching bra. All cotton separates were in keeping with the early seventies preference for natural fibers and colors.

Drawing by Kenneth Paul Block

Play it short

The advent of two color reproduction in *WWD* facilitated the dynamic artwork created in the seventies. In this illustration of Willi Smith's forties inspired short-set, Kenneth Paul Block (Kenneth) used color to offset the black and white garments and creates a sense of locale.

COLOR IT SPRING

In this illustration of hosiery and bodywear, Pedro Barrios's inventive manipulation of positive and negative space creates a pleasing layout. It recalls M. C. Escher's impossible structures and transformation prints. Barrios's use of size and overlapping figures suggests depth in his composition.

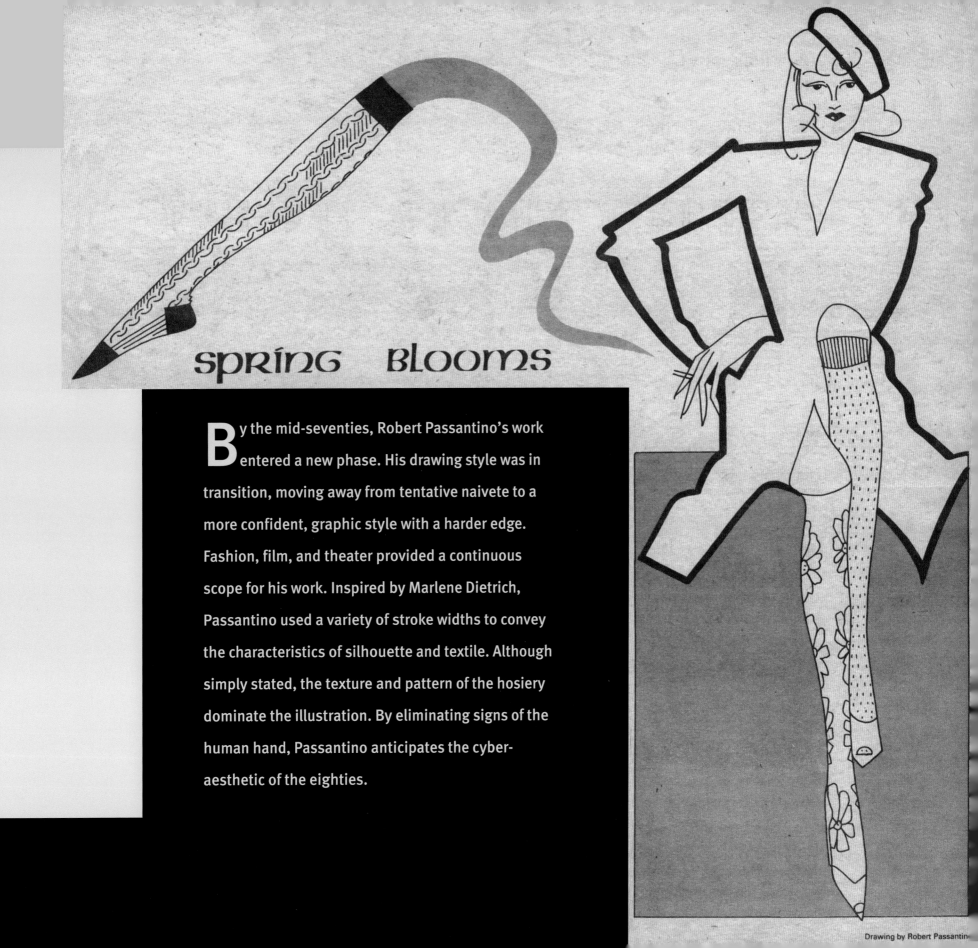

spring blooms

By the mid-seventies, Robert Passantino's work entered a new phase. His drawing style was in transition, moving away from tentative naivete to a more confident, graphic style with a harder edge. Fashion, film, and theater provided a continuous scope for his work. Inspired by Marlene Dietrich, Passantino used a variety of stroke widths to convey the characteristics of silhouette and textile. Although simply stated, the texture and pattern of the hosiery dominate the illustration. By eliminating signs of the human hand, Passantino anticipates the cyber-aesthetic of the eighties.

Drawing by Robert Passantino

Best of New York

For champagne sipping in your limo

Drawing by Glen Tunstull

G len Tunstull used his signature chiaroscuro effects to refashion the physical world according to a private vision of the glamorous disco culture.

Deborah Marquit's mural-like drawings also feature idiosyncratic scenarios of urban dramas. With uncertain energy resources and a flagging economy in the late seventies, even glamour girls had to rely on public transportation.

Drawing by Deborah Marquit

Designer Perry Ellis suggests showing several soft shapes in a crowded subway to get across the message.

Taking the 'A' train

Tennis had a high profile in 1973 after Billie Jean King defeated Bobby Riggs in a battle-of-the-sexes tournament. The spontaneity of Kenneth Paul Block's (Kenneth) drawing captures the fast action of tennis.

On the terry track: Jacquards

Charles Boone's photomontage prefigures the digital photoediting techniques of the nineties. By merging the figure with the frame, the visual boundary simultaneously joins and offsets the illustration with the rest of the page.

Drawing by CHARLES BOONE

In these drawings we begin to see the emergence of Steven Meisel's offbeat sensibilities. He used both precision and exaggeration to document the popularity of sweater dressing as it evolved with the development of lycra and spandex. Body conscious stretch clothing would be an integral crossover of active and fashion sportswear in the streetstyle of the eighties. The youthful sophisticates in these illustrations anticipate the arrival of punk and the cyberage.

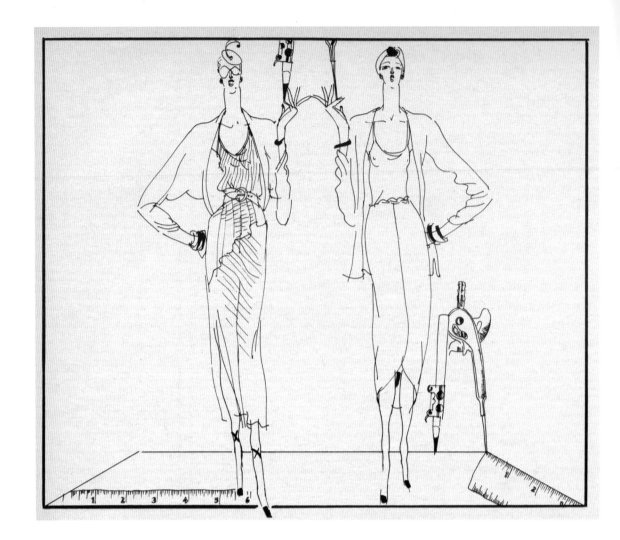

Drawings by STEVEN MEISEL

Pedro Barrios relied exclusively on linework to describe the flowing lines of this sweater and skirt. The soft drape is emphasized by a symmetrical pose and composition. Garment silhouettes became fuller and more luxurious at the end of the seventies owing to the Eastern aesthetic and in anticipation of eighties' luxe.

Steven Stipelman's application of opaque paint on coloraid and craft paper creates a sense of immediate visual impression. Of all the *WWD* artists, his is perhaps the most subjective response to fashion.

TEXTALIA '77

a merchandising and advertising supplement to women's wear daily

may 1977
cover information on page 2
all drawings by steven stipelman

If you always use the same perfume, is it inevitable that you'll lose your ability to smell it?

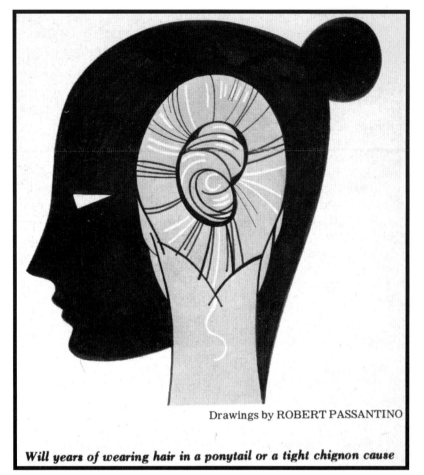

Drawings by ROBERT PASSANTINO

Will years of wearing hair in a ponytail or a tight chignon cause

In December 1977, Robert Passantino used his new graphic style to debunk beauty hits and myths.

Is wearing dark glasses, year-round, indoors and out, harmful to the eyes?

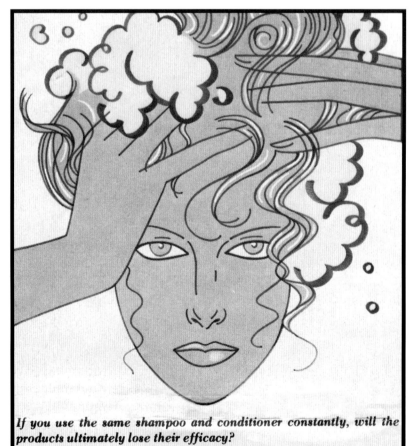

If you use the same shampoo and conditioner constantly, will the products ultimately lose their efficacy?

NOTES

1. Jonathan M. Woodham, *Twentieth Century Ornament* (New York: Rizzoli International Publications, 1990) p. 235.
2. Ibid., p. 254.
3. Ibid., pp. 237–238.
4. Mablen Jones, *Getting It On, The Clothing of Rock and Roll* (Abbeville Press, 1987), pp. 107–108.
5. Vicki Goldberg, "A Certain Look the Camera Sold," *The New York Times*, 18 November 2001, P. 37.
6. Woodham, *Twentieth Century Ornament*, pp. 274–275.
7. Raymond Cogniat, *Twentieth Cenutry Drawings and Watercolors* (New York: Crown Publishers).
8. Eunice Moore Sloane, *Illustrating Fashion, rev. ed.* (New York: Harper and Row, 1977), pp. 174–178.

WWD80s

"Some boys kiss me, some boys hug me

I think they're O.K.

If they don't give me proper credit

I just walk away

They can beg and they can plead

But they can't see the light, that's right

'Cause the boy with the cold hard cash

Is always Mister Right . . .

Material Girl

In 1980, the personal computer age was in its infancy and former hippies were flirting with middle age. The sixties' counterculture was adamant in their mistrust of anyone over the age of 30, but now the baby boomers were fast approaching this self-set benchmark. Science was impacting industry as the old technology of tubes and transistors was replaced by integrated circuitry. The consumer market was flooded with the results of ongoing and diverse product development. Self-organizing, nonlinear computer systems reinforced the overlapping and contradiction of trends. In the wake of relations between the superpowers, American corporations were moving across international boundaries as the ad hoc ambassadors of capitalism. Globalism and the widespread use of computer technologies set the stage for postmodernism and its irreverent mixing of different historical and cultural styles. The extended reach of corporate influence and an inequitable distribution of wealth antagonized the once-marginal punk movement into an explosion. The baby boom generation was still a force to be reckoned with in a self-perpetuating consumer culture. The emotional detachment that helped boomers survive the turbulent seventies was repositioned as an icy cool pose for the cyberage. Well into their adult years, they began to crave comforts and luxury. The consumerism they had spurned in prior decades was now embraced with a vengeance.

The eighties' celebration of affluence was a testament to marketing in the seventies: Consumers had been effectively conditioned to buy in excess. Recreational shopping was the norm in all income brackets as living patterns and aesthetics were shaped by the mass media. Baby boomers had been weaned on television, which made a vast array of material goods seem both familiar, accessible, and necessary. Many former hippies who had tried to effect change by working from within

the corporate structure had, instead, been seduced by attainable wealth. Women who pursued new career opportunities in the seventies had established positions of power by the eighties. Members of the "me" generation were newly tagged young urban professionals, or yuppies. In the days before "casual Fridays," yuppies climbing the corporate ladder were unabashedly dressed for success. Both men and women adopted a tasteful business style of dressing in suits designed by Georgio Armani, Ralph Lauren, Calvin Klein, and Donna Karan.[1] Exaggerated shoulder padding in jackets, blouses, and T-shirts was both a pastiche of forties' style and a symbol of a woman's empowerment in the eighties.

As seventies' hippies, the baby boomers had developed a reflexive disregard for untenable laws and corrupt authority figures. This habit carried over into the eighties as a not-so-well intentioned bending of the rules for personal enrichment. Yuppies turned a blind eye to questionable labor practices and environmental disasters abroad. Cocaine replaced LSD as the irresistible drug of choice. Imprudent financial transactions such as insider trading, leveraged buyouts, and the sale of junk bonds were wildly profitable and a source of disposable income. Baby boomers, who had subverted class structure in the sixties and the seventies, courted status and prestige in the eighties. Expenditures on luxuries and entertainment increased as yuppies reveled in hedonism that required new, outrageous expression. Brought together by new communication technologies, the global village lived vicariously through prime time soap operas such as *Dynasty* and *Dallas*. Seeds were planted for twenty-first-century reality TV with *Lifestyles of the Rich and Famous* and the televised royal wedding of Britain's Prince Charles and Lady Diana Spencer in 1981. Whereas Jackie Kennedy had been the fashion icon of democracy in the sixties, the world now looked at Princess Diana with an eye to snob appeal.

Equally significant influences from the street rose in opposition to the resurrection of elitism. Madonna, perhaps the most mercurial and fashion-savvy icon ever, burst onto the scene. She not only gave voice to the eighties' anthem for a "material world," but also was responsible for reintroducing the corset to a postfeminist generation. Picking up where Deborah Harry (of Blondie) left off, Madonna and Cindi Lauper upended the premise of erotic objectification in MTV parodies of Marilyn Monroe, the prototypical "dumb blonde."[2] As provocative sex objects, the bad girls of rock and roll were, paradoxically, in control. Their postmodern lyrics could be interpreted with or without irony, as either acceptance or rejection of a feminist stance and hedonistic materialism.

As part of the eighties' rebound in societal trends, a conservative political swing grew out of pro-business sentiment in an inflated economy. President Jimmy Carter was unsuccessful in his second bid for office when American voters elected Republican Ronald Reagan in 1980. President Reagan supported downsizing of the federal government and corporate deregulation, as well as less-restrictive gun control.

As a staunch anticommunist, Reagan was determined to end the cold war on his watch. Economic forces expedited Reagan's mandate to stamp out communism. Capitalism was spreading the consumer economy throughout the world, courtesy of multinational corporations. In the Soviet Union, President Mikhail Gorbachev began to realize that the economics of communism were not sustainable. Gorbachev championed a comingling of the capitalist and communist economic systems and pushed for détente with the United States. A movement to democratize the People's Republic of China was also gaining momentum.

Closer to home, Americans focused on pressing domestic issues at hand. Public opinion favored a sweeping revision of the U.S. tax code. The 1987 Senate investigation of the Reagan administration's secret initiatives, known as the Iran-Contra scandal, polarized public opinion. As in the seventies, Americans had to once again evaluate their definition of patriotism. The eighties also brought a less-equitable distribution of wealth and, as a consequence, a distinct class bias in access to technology. With consumer markets no longer defined solely by national boundaries, the American economy was quickly being reconfigured to take advantage of globalization. The number of well-paying manufacturing jobs had been declining since the seventies, leaving many people disenchanted and unemployed. A second paycheck in the family was no longer a luxury, and women whose career ambitions were initially motivated by self-actualization found themselves working out of necessity. The shrinking middle class struggled for survival in the face of growing corporate influence.

Aggravated malcontent fostered the early punk

movement in New York. By the late seventies punk was exported to Britain, where it tore away at the veneer of British aristocracy. Exploding amid the dire economic situation, British punk was more subversive and confrontational than its American progenitor. At the heart of McClaren's successful promotion of the Sex Pistols was the shock value of an extreme visual style. McClaren's collaboration with designer Westwood set a new precedent for the fusion of art rock, fashion, and marketing. On December 7, 1977, *WWD* proclaimed, "It's only rock and roll, but you wear it!"

Punk was exported back to New York City in a virulent new form in the eighties. The revitalization of the punk scene restored an edginess to the counterculture. Its raw aesthetic was incorporated into graffiti tags, the random use of numbers and letters in surface designs, and crude vanity publications called fanzines.[3] Punk turned the concept of beauty upside down, celebrating deviance and

ugliness. A traditional sense of femininity was also upended as punk women donned combat boots, fishnet stockings, vinyl, rubber, and leather garments. Punk attire would go on to become an antifashion classic, an equally timeless alternative to the preppy look.

The fashion ideas taken up by the masses were increasingly those that stressed street style. Young, avant-garde designers such as Westwood and Jean-Paul Gaultier worked in opposition to the tasteful style adopted by the affluent business class. Ready-to-wear followed couture in a diluted appropriation of punk. Seventh Avenue favored motorcycle jackets, tartan kilts, and declawed bondage looks in black, the new year-round color of choice. A continuing Asian influence caused sportswear to soften and move away from the body, blurring the line between loungewear and sportswear. The concept of inside out ruled fashion in the color-blocked aerobic looks worn on the street. Responding to the influences of MTV and postfeminist doctrine, women incorporated lingerie into their decadent new street wear. Luxurious bras and camisoles peaking out of pin-striped power suits were feminine counterpoints to changing gender roles.

Punk was not the only significant movement to come from the street. The parallel evolution of hip-hop in the African-American community had an enormous impact on the popular culture of the eighties. Over the years, a sense of "cool" had grown out of the struggle for racial equality.[4] The alternative hip-hop and punk movements were on converging paths. By 1980, Rock Steady Crew was the first crossover act to perform at punk venues such as the Mudd Club. Rap music and break dancing were integral to the thriving hip-hop culture. Graffiti art, also born of the movement, by artists Jean Michel Basquiat, Keith Haring, and Kenny Scharf became a high ticket commodity in the eighties' contemporary art scene. Recognizing hip-hop's potential, corporate America began catering to "urban" sensibilities in fashion and music.

Branding was integral to eighties' fashion, coincidentally important to both hip-hop and yuppie styles. The hip-hop dress code called for running suits and shoes with either the revitalized Adidas stripe or Nike swoosh, Kangol caps, and oversized gold logo jewelry. Licensing continued to flourish, as designer labels turned utilitarian items such as jeans and bed linens into symbols of status. Gradually, marketing rather than ingenuity came to determine a fashion designer's success. Nineteen eighty-three marked the beginning of the end for Halston with the launch of his budget collection, designed exclusively for JCPenney. On the first day Halston's garments shipped to JCPenney's, Bergdorf Goodman dropped his designer collection. Having sold the Halston brand to Norton Simon in the seventies, the bankrupt designer could not even use his own name. Other fashion designers were able to achieve greater success with brand recognition. Affecting the appearance of landed gentry in his advertisements, Ralph Lauren began marketing lifestyle rather than fashion. Donna Karan, who started her own collection in 1985, was the first designer to openly acknowledge fashion's impossible body standards. Because Karan's softer power dressing was aimed at real women, her new venture was an ongoing success. Many designers began marketing second, more afford-able "bridge" collections that spanned the gap between designer and moderate price points.

The continued revitalization of haute couture was fueled by the reemergence of an elite class. Avant-garde fashion designers attending to the needs of their new patrons upended the haute couture. Christian Lacroix's pairing of the "pouf" and the corset was well suited to eighties' extrava-

gance. In 1983, Karl Lagerfeld was enlisted to reinterpret the house of Chanel for modern lifestyles. Azzedine Alaïa used new stretch fiber technology for silhouettes that hugged and shaped the body. The 1979 Alta Moda exposition held in Milan set the stage for Italian designers Georgio Armani, Gianni Versace, Gianfranco Ferré, Valentino, and Krizia in the eighties. A new group of fashion designers, hailing from Belgium, also emerged. Known as the Antwerp Six, Ann Demeulemeester, Dries Van Noten, Martin Margiela, Josephus Thimister, Dirk Bikkemberg, and Walter Van Beirendonck began working in the spirit of deconstructivism first introduced by the more conceptual Japanese designers. Their creations were a wry commentary on traditional garment construction. With its intentional tears and exposed seam allowances, deconstructivism was the fashion industry's inside joke.

This sense of detachment and discontinuity grew out of transcending physical limits in cyberspace and had direct correspondence to many postmodern movements. Reinterpretations of the past served as a commentary on the present, with a strong emphasis on parody, pastiche, and deconstruction. The preservation movements of the seventies had helped to heighten awareness of the ornamental features from earlier times. As a result of a Supreme Court ruling in 1978, designated landmarks such as New York City's Grand Central Station were rescued from the wrecking ball. New structures featured the utility of modern design combined with other 20th-century styles. In the world of hip-hop, musicians similarly "sampled" and recombined sound bites from the past.

As hardware was miniaturized and software expanded in the eighties, affordable personal computers became a reality. The advent of cyberspace provided new ways to organize and disseminate knowledge. Postmodernists asserted that in the future, anything that could not be

digitized would cease to be knowledge. Science fiction writer William Gibson spawned an entire cyberpunk subculture based on the future role of computer hackers in society. Gibson's speculation about a brain-computer interface anticipated the nineties' techno-rave subculture and experiments with virtual reality. By 1984, Gibson's ideas were reflected on MTV in the creation of Max Headroom, the first cyborg veejay. Art rock musicians such as DEVO, Laurie Anderson, and the Talking Heads began referencing science fiction in their affectation of droidlike personas.

Movies and television continued to shape the nature of experience, and began to feature high-fashion clothing and rock-and-roll soundtracks. Don Johnson's role on the TV series *Miami Vice* earned him the type of celebrity status previously reserved for rock stars. The catch phrase "as seen on MTV" lent new credibility to just about anything, and the digitally enhanced television

E. Sottsass, "Carlton"
(Room Divider)
Memphis, 1981.
Courtesy, Memphis,
S.R.L. Reprinted with
permission.

revolted against corporate influences. Newly launched magazines such as *Wired* and *iD* featured socially relevant, groundbreaking visuals. Proponents of the "new wave" used idiosyncratic color, experimental typography, and found images as a rejection of highbrow theory and tasteful elitism.[5] A sense of the human hand was used in counterpoint to the consumer culture and corresponded to the growing popularity of outsider or naive art.

In the postmodern eighties, everything new seemed old again. New technology afforded state-of-the-art faux finishes, which created the illusion of distressed and weathered surfaces. Paralleling movements in art and architecture, fashion designers created retro-romantic looks by mixing and matching different historical elements.

The cross-pollination of fashion and art intensified throughout the eighties. The experiments of the Memphis design group, in Milan, were evident in the unconventional incorporation of grids,

appearances seemed to become more powerful than the experience of live performance.

An anti-style movement erupted in graphic design, similar to the nihilism manifested in the popular culture as punk. Vanguard art directors and illustrators, such as Tibor and Maira Kalman, dots, and confetti shapes in all kinds of surface design. Ongoing fashion influences from the East caused garments to become more conceptual. Japanese designers Yamamoto, Kansai, Miyake, and Kawabuko all had strong relationships with the visual and performing arts community. In 1980, Miyake took the fusion of art and fashion to a new level in the creation of wearable art pieces such as molded plastic body corsets. Saint Laurent, who had previously established a signature style of referencing fine art, continued in this vein with his 1981 Matisse collection.

The evolving cyberaesthetic reinforced a cultural preference for photographic images in and beyond the commercial arena. Having found new acceptance in the world of fine art, photography was introducing elements of fashion and courting controversy in this new arena. Cindy Sherman's self-portraits challenged the images and myths of the popular culture. Sherman blurred the boundaries between fashion and art by using makeup

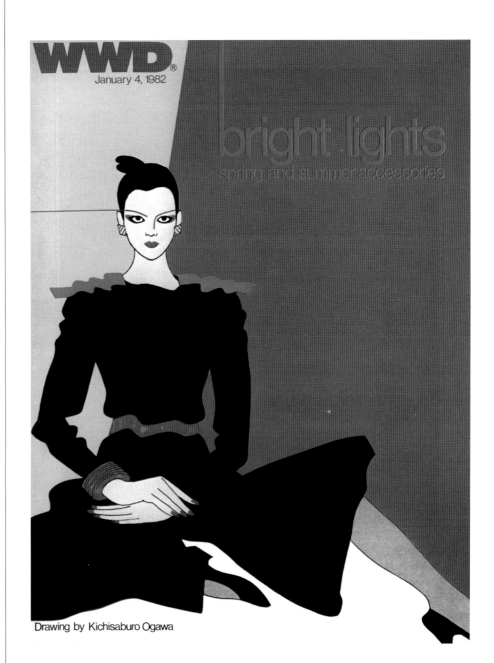

Drawing by Kichisaburo Ogawa

Henri Matisse, *The Toboggan*. From the Jazz series, June 1943. Photo: Adam Rzepka. © Copyright succession H. Matisse/ARS, NY. Musée National d'Art Moderne, Centre Georges Pompidou, Paris, France. Copyright CNAC/MNAM/ Dist. Réunion des Musées Nationaux/Art Resource, NY. Reprinted with permission.

and costume to imitate B movies and classic paintings. Robert Mapplethorpe stirred even greater controversy by using art deco style to examine sadomasochism in the homosexual sub-culture. Front-page news of Rock Hudson's AIDS-related death in 1985 cast an additional pall over Mapplethorpe's work. Heightened public aware-ness of the AIDS epidemic put a damper on the hedonism of the early eighties and triggered an austere backlash that was reinforced by the 1987 stock market crash.

The art direction at *WWD* underwent a notice-able change in the eighties. Layouts on page one began to feature a single figure with minimal copy. Larger and more powerful images featured throughout the publication advanced the content of the text. In consideration of the populist fashion philosophy first advanced by Donna Karan, the figures used to illustrate the softer power dressing reflected more realistic adult proportions. Bold stances conveyed postfeminist attitudes, celebrating a woman's dual empower-ment in the boardroom and the bedroom, with a cross-pollination of costumes for both. Gestures became robotic to correspond with the detach-ment and dissociation of cyberpunk. Reflecting the gradual homogenization of world cultures, distinct racial diversity in the layouts was barely discernible. The lavish extravagence of the eighties was represented in the illustrations by way of location, narrative, and in the garments themselves.

The referencing of fine art movements from the past was limited, in keeping with the post-modern avoidance of nostalgia in its purest form. Although the *WWD* layouts continued to parallel trends in the contemporary arts, they did so to a lesser extent as the fine art world turned away from representational painting towards neoexpressionism, graffiti art, and photography. As a result, the converging paths of illustration and photography began to intersect. Prevailing styles in the applied arts continued to be influential. Layouts featured Memphis-inspired graphics, as seen on MTV. The anti-style fusion of hand-rendered text and illustration corresponded to new wave graphic design sensibilities. A respectful similarity existed between the *WWD* illustrations and the poster art of the Paul Davis

Paul Davis, *China Seas*
poster. Courtesy, ©
2003 Paul Davis.

Studio. The impact of the 1985 republication of
Matisse's "Jazz" series was also apparent. At about
this time, Robert Passantino, always a lightening
rod for change, began experimenting with cut
paper collage. Even his flat application of paint
or pastel suggests the effect of cut paper. By
prioritizing mass over line, Passantino introduced
a new level of abstraction to his illustrations that

was suited to the more conceptual fashion of the
eighties.

Beginning in the late seventies, *WWD* began to
include supplements dedicated to specific garment
categories or markets as a periodic addendum to
daily publication. Supplements such as *Best of New
York* featured higher production values and a vast
array of clothing by multiple fashion designers. A
consistent relationship between the garments in
serial compositions was established by theme and
drawing style. Illustrations of the different *WWD*
categories were assigned according to each artist's
unique visual persona. Kenneth and Stipelman
had an elegant, rapid notation style that was well
suited to the late-breaking news of luxurious
haute couture. Boone and Young, who displayed a
similar style and spirit, often worked in tandem
on multipage supplements devoted to high-
fashion sportswear. The graphic precision and
athleticism of their figure proportions made

Ogawa and Passantino the right team for active and coordinated sportswear. Clayton Purnell and Marquit documented the redesign of lingerie and bridal wear for a postfeminist generation. Clayton Purnell's dreamlike tableaus took on added dimension in the eighties with the use of context and props such as musical instruments and seashells. Although the reader is drawn in by an imaginative fantasy, the story and her ethereal figures never overwhelm the clothing.

Influenced by the unorthodox style of new wave graphic design, the *WWD* illustrators sought out new solutions to avoid formulaic layouts. One artist's experiment invariably influenced another's work. New techniques occasionally evolved by accident, but more often occurred in conjunction with changing fashion. As romanticism softened garment silhouettes, the *WWD* illustrators began to consider new media choices for conveying increased volume and luxurious fabrics. By the

Seaworthy

end of the decade even Passantino and Ogawa, artists with more graphic leanings, used soft brush or pencil lines to describe luxe jersey looks and the "pouf." The character of their line was determined by the surface of the paper. Such evidence of the hand distinguished the artists' drawings from photography and slick graphic reproduction. Boundaries between text and art were blurred in the fusion of illustration and hand-rendered headlines. As a consequence of the new design dictates, *WWD* was invested with a renewed vitality and spontaneity.

Viewed in hindsight, the illustrations from this period are less derivative and more straightforward in their description of fashion. Change came as a result of subtle experimentation with scale and media. Influenced by a shared cyberaesthetic, editorial and fine art content continued to dovetail into the nineties. The preference for photography in both fields would cause the four remaining staff illustrators (Kenneth, Stipelman, Passantino, and Ogawa) to play a diminishing role at *WWD*.

Power suits began appearing at the new bridge price point early in the eighties. Taking a cue from men's wear, shoulder lines were exaggerated by the addition of padding. Feminizing tucks and shirring were also added for dramatic shoulder presence. Robert Passantino carried over stylistic elements from the seventies, but they were newly combined with his use of pattern in tightly constructed layouts. He employed the conventions of cartoon art, suggesting robotic motion through calculation rather than spontaneity.

More extreme versions of the "power suit" by avant-garde designers such as Claude Montana and Thierry Mugler featured domination, military, and sci-fi looks. Robert Passantino modified his figure proportion to correspond with the empowered postfeminist and her tough urban chic. His adult women are less elongated and more powerfully built than in past years.

In these illustrations by Robert Young, the women seem to be frozen in time, caught in the act of walking the dog or hailing a taxi. Eighties' career dressing featured jackets layered over knee-length skirts in fabrications that referenced both men's suiting and punk. Pussycat bows feminized the tradition of Windsor-knotted ties in the workplace.

Drawing by ROBERT YOUNG

March 4, 1985

Drawing by KENNETH PAUL BLOCK

BILL BLASS's contradictory seven-eighths coat in sporty doublefaced wool plaid bordered with luxurious sable

These illustrations utilize opaque paint on colored backgrounds and indicate the reciprocal influence between Kenneth Paul Block (Kenneth) (*this page*) and Steven Stipelman (*opposite*). Kenneth, Stipelman, Robert Young and Charles Boone would reliably channel their vision of eighties fashion through immediate and expressive media. The artists with more graphic leanings, such as Kichisaburo Ogawa and Robert Passantino, relied on calculated and hard-edge methods of representation.

Swept Away

Drawing by Steven Stipelman

In these illustrations, Steven Stipelman combined the delicacy of fine penwork with a bold, dry brush technique to offset the luxurious volume and texture of blanket-like outerwear.

Drawing by STEVEN STIPELMAN

Best of New York

BEST of NEW YORK

Barely-there bandeaus and Madonna-inspired brassiere tops offer a youthfully sexy counterpoint to resort's curvaceous but covered-up looks.

BETSY GONZALEZ accents her hot pink silk cloque jacket and high-waist trousers with a green silk crepe bra.

MICHAEL KORS slips a skinny white cotton bandeau under his navy linen jacket and matching pleated trousers.

DANNY NOBLE teams a white brassiere with a long jacket and easy trousers, all in rayon faille.

Drawing by ROBERT YOUNG

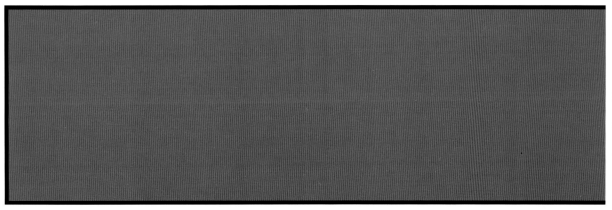

Robert Young's illustration uses the impressionistic conventions of traditional fashion art, but in a modified form to accommodate contemporary customer profile and garment silhouette. Donna Karan's oversized silhouettes implied both importance and luxury for all figure types (*opposite*). Here, a voluminous silhouette is illustrated using a single figure on the all-important "page one."

FASHION OUTLOOK 85

WWD

WOMEN'S WEAR DAILY   VOL. 148 NO. 118
WEDNESDAY, DECEMBER 19, 1984   50 Cents

DONNA KARAN

NEW YORK — Donna Karan's penchant for layers of luxury separates characterizes her first independent collection for fall '85. Here, the designer swathes an elongated cashmere turtleneck and "the essential short black skirt" in layers of cashmere — a taupe shell envelops another in gold, accented by a wool and cashmere scarf.

MACY'S CALIF.

Kahn to succeed Schlein

NEW YORK — Harold Kahn, president of R.H. Macy & Co.'s Davison's in Atlanta, has been named chairman and chief executive officer of the San Francisco-based Macy's California division, succeeding Philip S. Schlein, who resigned.

The move, which takes effect Feb. 1, was announced by R.H. Macy late Tuesday.

When reached in his San Francisco office, Schlein said he had no comment. Reports are circulating that Schlein may be going to take a post with

See KAHN, page 17

Drawing by CHARLES BOONE

1 7 3

INSIDE OUT

NEW YORK — The femme fatale provides inspiration for the season's innerwear that's too sizzling to limit to the boudoir. Looks range from Natori's dramatic number, inspired by "La Bohème," to Hanky Panky's altar-ready bustier cascading in flowers. Here, some of the looks that will surface to heat up holiday nights.

Flora Nikrooz's curve-flattering sequined black bustier in cotton and nylon French lace (upper left); Hanky Panky's structured rose pink bustier accented with green and magenta flowers, all in suede

Natori's red cotton and acetate moire bustier with black velvet appliques (left); Lucine Almas Original's Indian-print silk brocade bustier in gold, red and green at Judy Mercer

Lingerie had brand-new appeal to a postfeminist generation. Having spurned their bras in the sixties, women now chose expensive foundations and lingerie as a feminine counterpoint to power dressing. Luxurious undergarments were worn as postmodern decadent street wear.

Deborah Marquit's unconventional poses of empowered women correspond to postfeminism in the disassociation of the cyberage. The reinterpretation of Victorian and art deco looks for intimate apparel was in keeping with the eighties' view of romanticism. Marquit's experience as a *WWD* illustrator laid the groundwork for her later success as a designer of lingerie.

Drawing by Deborah Marquit

Charles Boone's modern interpretation of traditional fashion art features a freer hand and realistic figure proportions. His drawing style is similar in spontaneity to that of Kenneth Paul Block (Kenneth), but is distinguished by casual, antifashion poses that provide the viewer with a glamorous reality check. The increased scale of the single, cropped figure places a greater emphasis on the quality of the artist's draftsmanship.

Drawing by CHARLES BOONE

Leggy to look at

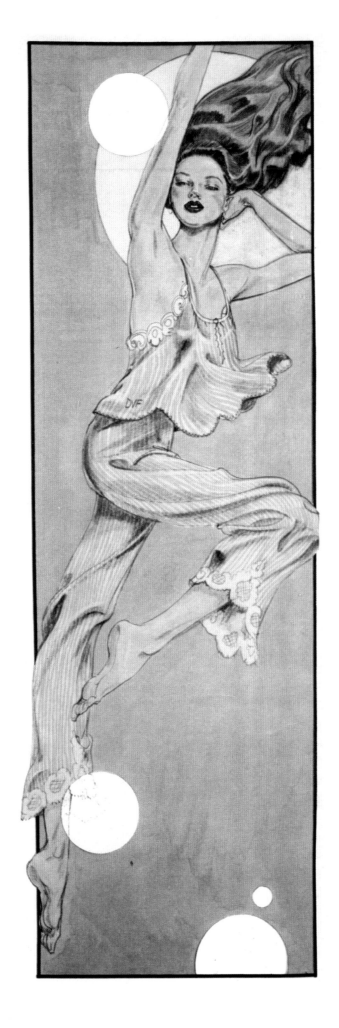

In contrast to her signature style of elaborate allegory, Catherine Clayton Purnell took an uncharacteristically graphic approach to these lingerie illustrations. It is possible that her atypical technique was a function of expediency in having to complete a multipage supplement on short notice.

GETTING ROMANTIC

October 25, 1984   *Trendsetters: Intimate apparel for spring*   *Drawing by Catherine Clayton Purnell*

The hyper reality of Catherine Clayton Purnell's idiosyncratic fantasies mirrors the precision of surrealism. As in all fairy tales, a certain measure of reality grounds the viewer and lends credibility to the fantasy.

Late fall intimate apparel

DREAM RICH

May 2, 1985
Drawing by Catherine Clayton Purnell

Ski lifts

The innovation of microfiber, polar fleece, and heat-molded seaming revolutionized performance apparel in the eighties. The tightly knit construction of these textiles gave the garments enhanced thermal and waterproof properties. The comfort and functionality of Patagonia's "gear" spawned a cult following during and after the eighties. The brushed high-tech fabrics utilized on ski slopes eventually trickled down to street wear as a style of versatile, athletic chic.

Drawings by CATHERINE CLAYTON PURNELL

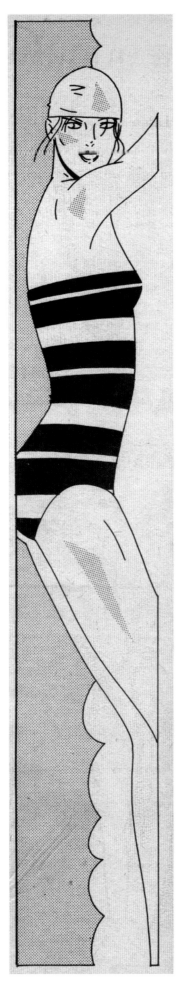

A new athleticism was apparent in the *WWD* layouts of the eighties. Sports enthusiasts focused their attention on female athletes such as three-time Olympic gold medallist Florence Griffith Joyner (Flo Jo). Flo Jo raised the profile of women who participated in sports. The introduction of brightly colored neoprene in Day-Glo wetsuits inspired color-blocked athletic fashion. Garments utilizing the science behind the wetsuit typified the eighties' high-tech fusion of technology and aesthetics.

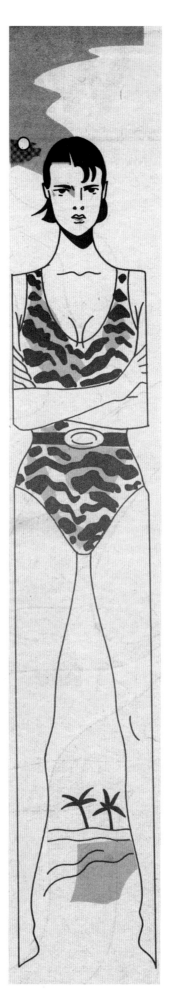

Seaworthy

Drawing by ROBERT PASSANTINO

There's a hard-edge sensuality to this season's industrial-influenced swimsuits.
Ariel's yellow Lycra spandex and nylon bikini is paired with a rubbery polyurethane skin-tight gray top. He adds a bright yellow industrial zipper for Haye Design, New York.
At Cole Jrs., Los Angeles, the black and red nylon and spandex suit has a wet-suit look with its super-lean fit and white zipper.

The use of shadow and light as graphic elements was one of the few constants in Robert Passantino's ongoing evolution. This inventive composition relies on a forced and ambiguous perspective. The inclusion of images that recall the trade routes of the China seas is evidence of a focus on the Pacific Rim.

In the eighties, women joined the craze for pumping iron and shaping powerful bodies with precision weight-training regimens. Seventh Avenue quickly knocked off Azzedine Alaïa's stretch couture for activewear looks. Norma Kamali and Donna Karan also began manufacturing coordinated separates made from spandex and Lycra which blurred the distinction between garment categories.

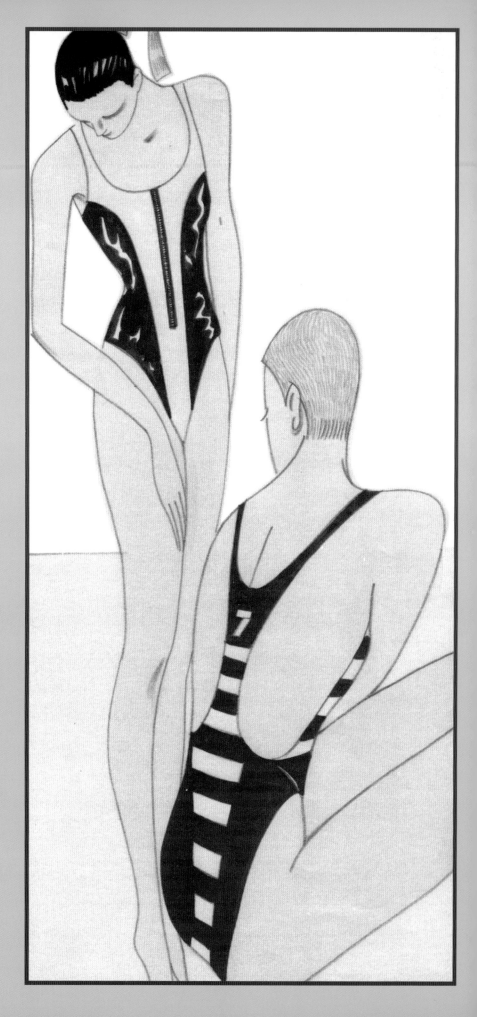

Television's impact on fashion is evident in the borrowing of MTV's Memphis-inspired graphics. These illustrations by Robert Passantino (*this page*) and Kenneth Paul Block (Kenneth) (*opposite*) demonstrate idiosyncratic surface design with their use of oversized polka dots and unconventional prints. Kenneth's inclusion of a baroque footstool is the perfect postmodern finishing touch.

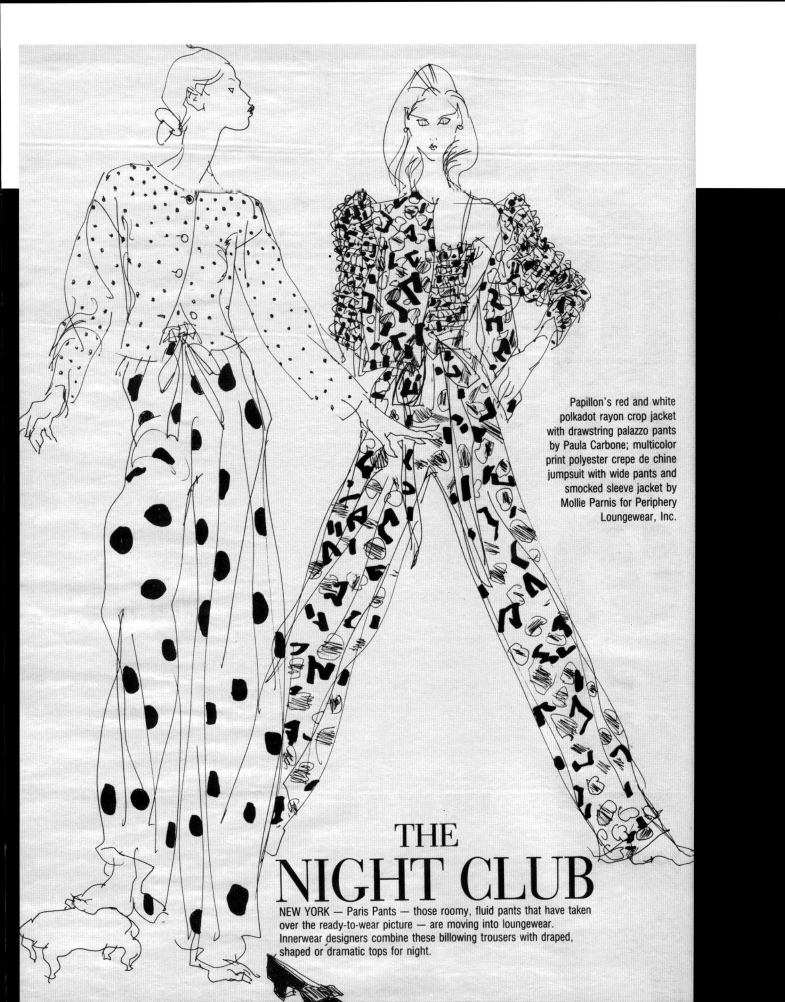

Papillon's red and white polkadot rayon crop jacket with drawstring palazzo pants by Paula Carbone; multicolor print polyester crepe de chine jumpsuit with wide pants and smocked sleeve jacket by Mollie Parnis for Periphery Loungewear, Inc.

THE
NIGHT CLUB

NEW YORK — Paris Pants — those roomy, fluid pants that have taken over the ready-to-wear picture — are moving into loungewear. Innerwear designers combine these billowing trousers with draped, shaped or dramatic tops for night.

Surface interest and gridlike graphic elements reflect Memphis design sensibilities and the discontinuity of the cyberaesthetic.

January 4, 1982

bright lights
spring and summer accessories

Kichisaburo Ogawa's flat application of bright color and confetti shapes reflect the eighties' new wave challenge to the concept of good taste.

Drawing by Kichisaburo Ogawa

NEW YORK — When the Metropolitan Museum of Art opens its Yves Saint Laurent retrospective with a press review and gala dinner on Dec. 5 (the official opening is Dec. 14), Yves watchers will be treated to a lush outpouring from the designer's vast oeuvre. Here, from the Picasso collection of spring-summer 1980 — among YSL's own favorites — the Gazar dress cape with neck ruffles, lent by Diana Vreeland.

YSL

In this illustration, Kenneth Paul Block's (Kenneth) bold, abstract forms mirror the cubism that inspired Yves Saint Laurent's Picasso Collection.

Drawing by KENNETH PAUL BLOCK

In 1983-84, the Metropolitan Museum of Art (MET) in New York honored Yves Saint Laurent with a retrospective exhibition and gala. For the first time the work of a living fashion designer was celebrated at the MET. *WWD* devoted a full-color supplement to an overview of Saint Laurent's revolutionary body of work. Highlights from the show included the Mondrian dress, the safari pantsuit, Le Smoking, and his Picasso collection.

Trapeze in strawberry linen, and in wool boucle, designed by YSL for Christian Dior, spring-summer, 1958; silk organza evening dress embroidered with wood beads and black plastic geometric appliques; spring-summer, 1967.

Black silk moire corselet and white cotton Bermuda shorts; spring-summer, 1977

Two-piece tailleur in wool pique jersey, fall-winter, 1969-70; silk taffeta evening dress, fall-winter, 1971-72

Yves Saint Laurent

Wool cocktail
dress, fall–
winter, 1962-63

...ool gabardine pantsuit, doubleknit wool jersey
...ket and jumpsuit, fall, winter, 1968–69; Silk satin
...mock and gray velvet skirt, fall–winter, 1962-63

Wool pique jersey Mondrian dress,
fall–winter, 1965-66; Pop art dress
in wool pique jersey, fall–winter 66-67

Silk ottoman cape;
fall–winter, 1983-84

Drawings by KENNETH
PAUL BLOCK

Over the years both the public and the press had responded to Saint Laurent's design innovations with enthusiasm. Not long after this exhibition, Saint Laurent disavowed fashion's mandate for seasonal reinvention. Instead, he pursued ongoing and continuous design development until his retirement in 2003.[6]

In 1980, Malcom McClaren and Vivienne Westwood launched the trend for "New Romantics" by outfitting art rocker Adam Ant as a pirate. On March 26, 1985, McClaren explained his intended irony to *WWD*:

> In London at that time, people were taping off the radios instead of buying records. I was in the process of thinking about Adam, what to do for the band, when it hit me, these people were modern pirates, stealing from their own culture. I thought the concept of pirates was perfect . . .

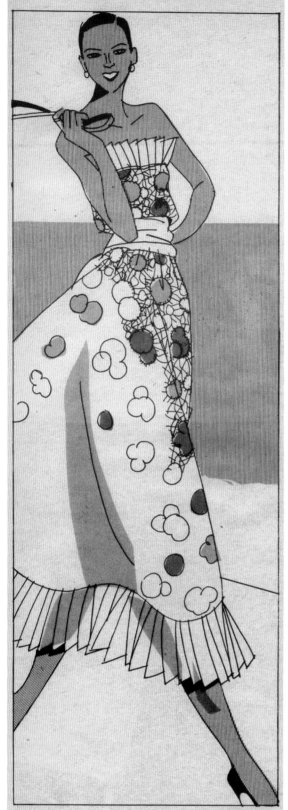

Summer's fanciful ballgowns explode into a burst of airy color.

ALBERT CAPRARO's bright bouquet of balloons works painted lace over full-skirted organza.

Seventh Avenue quickly adapted the "New Romantics" introduced by Vivienne Westwood and Malcolm McClaren. Ornament and accessories created additional volume in these luxurious silhouettes.

The FIT-makers' favorite flourish, the peplum, shows up at cocktail hour in flirtatiously ruffled silks.

HANAE MORI shapes boldly dotted black and white shadow-striped organza into a floral topped peplum blouse, with a narrow black silk skirt underneath.

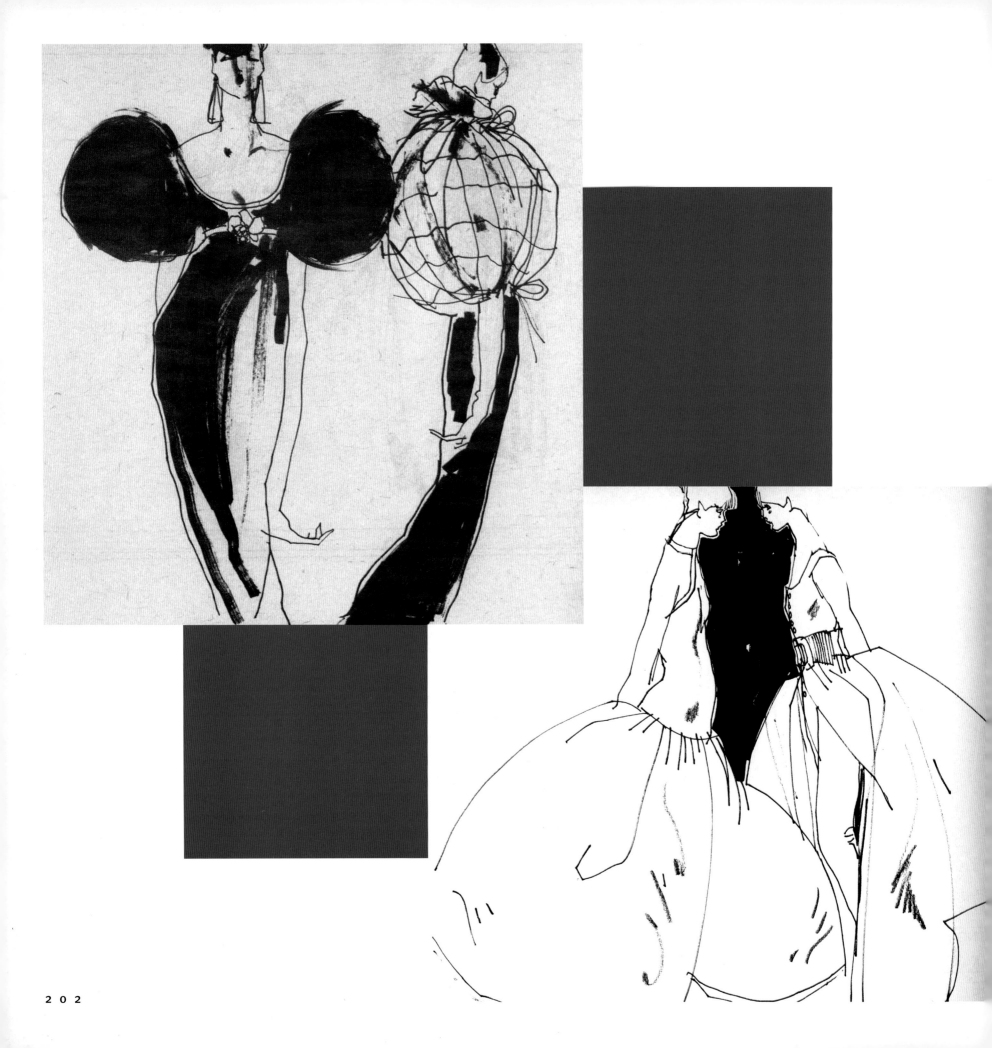

Form did not follow function in the eighties, as seen by the addition of decorative flounces, ruffles, bows, and oversized ricrac trim. Maximizing silhouettes, such as Christian Lacroix's "pouf," suggested both luxury and parody.

Boutique concepts: Maximizing trends

Drawing by ROBERT PASSANTINO

In 1986, Robert Passantino was experimenting with brush techniques to convey the softness and volume of silhouettes. His work at the end of the decade was less mechanized, indicating a return to impressionistic spontaneity.

A Classic Touch

PARIS — Some of Europe's finest accessories are in the most classic of modes for early fall. Delicately puffed gloves, bowed hats and tasseled bags add instant glamor to day or evening finery while golden baubles cast a shimmery glow.

Black felt bowed picture hat by MARIE MERCIER, goldplate hoop earrings by CHRISTIAN DIOR, black suede glove with puffed cuff by PHILIPPE MODEL.

DRAWING BY ROBERT PASSANTINO

Fichu necklines, an eighteenth century pastiche, provided softer accentuation of the shoulderline.

Offset by "power shoulders," Kichisaburo Ogawa illustrated ornamental jewelry and belts, which underscored eighties' luxe.

From pillbox to pirate hats, the millinery industry experienced a resurgence in the eighties. Hats, gloves, and other accessories became pivotal to postmodern fashion.

Kichisaburo Ogawa's illustration recalls the limited edition serigraph prints which were popular in the eighties.

210

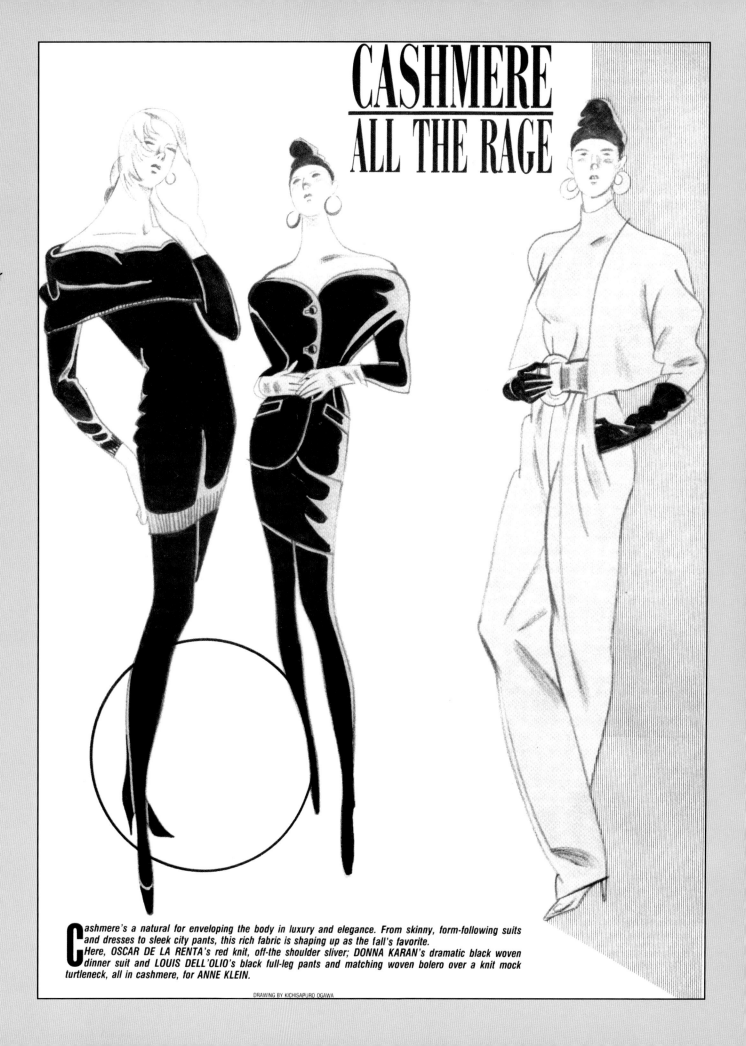

CASHMERE ALL THE RAGE

Cashmere was the ultimate look for luxurious and comfortable power dressing. Knitwear silhouettes, softened by off the shoulder and heart shape necklines, referenced the couture designs of Charles James. James blazed a trail for postmodern fashion throughout the thirties, forties, and fifties with his artful pastiche of historical styles.

Cashmere's a natural for enveloping the body in luxury and elegance. From skinny, form-following suits and dresses to sleek city pants, this rich fabric is shaping up as the fall's favorite. Here, OSCAR DE LA RENTA's red knit, off-the shoulder sliver; DONNA KARAN's dramatic black woven dinner suit and LOUIS DELL'OLIO's black full-leg pants and matching woven bolero over a knit mock turtleneck, all in cashmere, for ANNE KLEIN.

DRAWING BY KICHISABURO OGAWA

6

WOMEN'S WEAR DAILY, MONDAY, JANUARY 5, 1987

Summer's spirit is one of ease — the simplicity of a breezy T-shirt dress, the comfort of sleek terry cloth playclothes, the classic tradition of a relaxed blazer and trousers. Even for dressed-up days or nights, the look is clean and crisp, with an emphasis on the waist that underscores the season's femininity. Here, a look at the mood to come.

•

This page, from left: RALPH LAUREN's wool gabardine jacket over a rayon matte jersey wrap top and linen trousers; CAROLYNE ROEHM's long wool gabardine wrap dress and her sweet cotton crinoline look; PATRICIA PASTOR and JED KRASCELLA's flowing silk crepe dress for PERRY ELLIS

•

Opposite page, from left: OSCAR DE LA RENTA's trio of crisp linen dresses over cotton petticoats; DONNA KARAN's sexy cotton terrycloth looks

Drawing by
KENNETH PAUL BLOCK

BEST OF

Feminine sportswear
coordinates and
dresses were soft
counterpoints to the
hard edge power dress-
ing in the eighties.
T-shirt dresses and
terrycloth playclothes
epitomized the
crossover between
active and fashion
sportswear.

NEW YORK

SOME LIKE IT HOT

SECTION II
RESORT SWIMWEAR
COVER INFORMATION ON PAGE 2
DRAWING BY KENNETH PAUL BLOCK

The trend for color-blocked aerobic wear carried over to swimwear design with emphasis on drapery and asymmetric details.

ON THE BEACH
Summer is here, with its prickly hot days and languid nights. Don't get caught without the perfect swimsuit to wear to the beach. Here, one of the hottest sizzlers around — a blood red beauty with glamor girl allure from Norma Kamali.

By the end of the eighties, fashion illustration became increasingly abstract and was characterized by flattened shapes.

WIDE
APPEAL

...ANS AND CASUAL PANTS   NOVEMBER 8, 1983 DRAWING BY STEVEN STIPELMAN

The elimination of details in eighties' fashion sketches was thought to create a "wide appeal." Ultimately, the *WWD* artists had to fall back on traditional methods of fashion illustration in order to fulfill trade journalism's requirements. Steven Stipelman's illustration reflects a painterly approach and achieves a greater level of abstraction.

WWD

FALL TOPS AND BOTTOMS
MAY 6, 1987

A SUPPLEMENT TO WOMEN'S WEAR DAILY

COLLAGE BY ROBERT PASSANTINO

SHORT STORY

VANDA MAZZEO's red wool jersey trapeze dress; CORINNE DELEMAZURE's cropped sweater and high-waist pants in black wool, for SANS TAMBOURS NI TROMPETTES

Robert Passantino's experimentation with cut and torn paper collage shows the influence of the Matisse Jazz series.

BEST OF NEW YORK

7

Fall's newest looks are short, but have an abundance of glamor. For day, the mood is clean-lined and crisp, rich in texture and color. At night, the mood is more frivolous and subtly sexy.

By the late eighties, after brief experimentation with other methods and media, Kenneth Paul Block (Kenneth) settled into a signature style that would remain unchanged for the remainder of his career at *WWD*. Any variation to his expressive drawing style can be attributed solely to the manipulation of scale and layout governed by the *WWD* art direction.

BEST OF NEW YORK

The subtlety of cashmere and wool jersey comes through for early fall as designers drape and wrap some of their favorite silhouettes in sinuous folds for smart days or seductive evenings. Shapes that cling make the most of a woman's body in elegant wraps or simple sheaths. Here, a look at early fall's hot knits.

Calvin Klein's seductive black cashmere sheath, trimmed in grosgrain

Bill Blass's simply wrapped and belted camel wool jersey dress

The continued influence of Charles James is apparent in the use of asymmetric drapery and bared shoulders. The separates in this illustration were considered suitable for both day and "after five" wear.

W

NEW YORK

Page one of the May 18, 1989 edition of *W,* represents a synthesis of design principles that evolved in the eighties. Hand-rendered type reinforces the anti design philosophy of the new wave. By the end of the decade, young fashion designers, such as Isaac Mizrahi, Steven Sprouse, and Anna Sui incorporated components of the punk uni-form with luxurious fabrics. This reinterpreta-tion resulted in innovative new collections.

ISAAC
King of the Tartans

NEW YORK — Isaac Mizrahi showed the fashion world he's no flash in the pan. Supported by his terrific tartans, the 27-year-old Mizrahi scored yet another triumph (his third in a row). Here, one of his distinctive homages to the Highlands, the Royal Stewart cashmere kilt dress, under a cropped black and white silk taffeta gingham parka that would startle most clansmen. More from New York on pages 26 to 37.

SKETCH BY KENNETH PAUL BLOCK

SECOND CLASS POSTAGE PAID AT NEW YORK, NY
AND AT ADDITIONAL MAILING OFFICES

NOTES

1. Charlotte Seeling, *Fashion: The Century of the Designer, 1900–1999* (Konemann Verlagsgesellschaft).

2. Mablen Jones, *Getting It On, The Clothing of Rock and Roll* (Abbeville Press, 1987), pp. 153–154.

3. Jonathan M. Woodham, *Twentieth Century Ornament* (New York: Rizzoli International Publications, 1990), p. 243.

4. Jamel Shabazz and Ernie Paniccioli, *Back In The Days* (Powerhouse Books).

5. Liz Farrelly, *Tibor Kalman: Design Undesign* (The Ivy Press, 1998).

6. Charlotte Seeling, *Fashion: The Century of the Designer, 1900–1999* (Konemann Verlagsgesellschaft), p. 365.

WWD90s

"I started doing something at the end of its history."

Kenneth Paul Block

With the millennium fast approaching, the nineties was a period of transition. The early part of the decade saw a flurry of optimism and social conscience. Nelson Mandela was freed after more than 27 years of imprisonment in a South African jail, and the policy of apartheid was repealed shortly thereafter. Perestroika and the lifting of U.S. sanctions against the People's Republic of China formally ended the cold war, creating new players in the global economy.

On the domestic front, consumer confidence was undermined by the first Gulf War and finite domestic energy resources. A failing American economy caused the political pendulum to swing from the conservatism of the Reagan-Bush years to the liberalism of the Clinton administration. Beginning in the sixties with the Nixon-Kennedy debates, the outcome of presidential elections was determined by the molding of popular opinion on television. What was once considered a "photo op" became a media extravaganza in the nineties. Footage of sensational events, such as the police pursuit of O. J. Simpson, was played and replayed on both network and cable TV stations. CNN replaced radio as the ultimate, up-to-the-minute 24-hour news source. Having successfully "rocked the vote" on MTV, Bill Clinton was the first baby boomer to be inaugurated president in the new era of political correctness. Austere economic conditions prompted a noticeable shift to more discrete buying patterns. Preoccupation with appearance remained, but the social prestige of having the right look was now perceived as a politically incorrect embarrassment. In the nineties, comfort and convenience were paramount.

A stripped-down aesthetic evolved in response to the tough financial times. Grunge, the anti-fashion fusion of nihilistic punk and nostalgic hippie styles, had been a disaster on the runway. Minimalism was a welcome departure from this ill-considered trend. Proponents of a new understatement, such as Calvin Klein and Jil Sander, eliminated all accessories with the single exception of utilitarian sunglasses. A zenlike distillation of design elements reflected the ongoing influence of the Asian aesthetic. Swathing afforded a sense of safety in the midst of premillennium jitters and growing concern about the impact of technology. A new generation of performance fabrics enhanced with thermoactive, antibacterial, and UV-resistant properties provided added protection from the elements. The innovation of fiber optics facilitated the weaving of communication technologies directly into the warp and weft of new experimental textiles.

The diplomacy that precipitated the end of the cold war initiated a wave of international contracting and corporate expansion. As the global economy created bigger businesses and relatively greater risk, design innovation was subordinated to the marketing of utilitarian silhouettes.

American basics in keeping with the stripped-down domestic aesthetic were perceived to be exotic abroad. The iconic stars and stripes were incorporated into logos to enhance brand recognition. In making the ordinary fashionable, Tommy Hilfiger became a multimillionaire. Retail consolidation and economic recession contributed to the bankruptcy of the Federated and Allied buying offices. Financial experts took the helm from creative merchandising executives at department stores such as Barney's and Macy's. Charivari, a prestigious chain of high-fashion boutiques, also went belly-up. *WWD* itself became part of a larger business concern. The family-owned Fairchild Publications had been purchased by the publicly owned Capital Cities Broadcasting in 1968. In 1996, the Walt Disney Company acquired Capital Cities and Fairchild Publications along with it. By 1999, Fairchild became a part of the Newhouse media conglomerate, traded by Disney to Advance Publications.

The overall pace of social, cultural, and economic changes continued to be accelerated by technology. The debut of the World Wide Web created a new reliance on the Internet for commerce and the dissemination of information. The Web also afforded inexpensive access to an international client base, thereby leveling the playing field for small entrepreneurial businesses to compete against corporate giants. Fantastic dot-com business schemes inflated the salaries and expectations of generation X as they entered the job market. An evolving, disembodied cyberaesthetic grew out of the proliferation of computers in the home. Commonplace personal electronics played an increasing role in everyday life, yet mysteriously failed to save precious time. With the pace of life set to fast-forward, time became the new currency.[1] Women experienced the challenge of "having it all," juggling family and career in post-feminist times. Hillary Rodham Clinton redefined the role of first lady by maintaining an ongoing commitment to her own career. Unresolved issues surrounding gender identity were reflected in the popular culture through Cinderella-inspired fantasies such a *Pretty Woman* and a new feminization in women's apparel.

As genetic engineering became a reality, bioethicists examined the ramifications of cloning Dolly the sheep. Fantastic predictions of Armageddon in the year 2000 underscored an ambivalence to technology. In the decade-long prelude to the millennium, Y2K became the buzzword in a global community preoccupied with the possibility of computer failure as the date changed from 1999 to 2000. Extremists stockpiled essential supplies in anticipation of the havoc that might be wreaked if a system breakdown occurred. A less radical expression of this anxiety was a trend for "cocooning" in the home.[2] Interior design and at-home wear were given new emphasis. Full- and part-time telecommuting from home offices was on the rise. For those who ventured into the brick-and-mortar workplace, "casual Friday" attire evolved into the daily dress code. Electronic retail environments featured on the Home Shopping Network and the Internet brought virtual shopping directly to the consumer's doorstep.

The approaching millennium caused a continued wave of retro looks in all types of product design. Since the seventies, nostalgia had been a reliable selling tool, providing comfort for buyers in uncertain times. Postmodern design strategies were eventually called into question, regarded by some as a form of creative cannibalism. The information superhighway facilitated nearly simultaneous manufacturing of high-fashion knockoffs. The nineties' fashion industry was, to some extent, devouring itself.

To offset the dehumanization of technology, consumers began to advocate individuality. Fashion was subject to a greater level of personal interpretation by the customer. Anonymity was on the rise in overpopulated urban centers and the isolation of the suburbs. As manufacturers placed greater emphasis on focus groups and marketing, consumers became active participants in the design process. The success of megamarts such as Target and Kmart was built on vertical manufacturing and the preceived value of well-priced merchandise.

Fashion designers continued to enjoy cult status as celebrity CEOs. By the nineties, American fashion designers not only had achieved credibility in the global fashion arena, but were seen as leading the way. Tom Ford appeared on the scene, rocking the fashion world as he steered Gucci in a new creative direction. His success in rejuvenating the brand inspired a changing of the guard at other older fashion houses. IPOs, private-label manufacturing, and corporate expansion caused the fashion industry to become a multi-divisional corporate system. The measure of success for a young, entrepreneurial fashion designer was the absorption of his/her small thriving business by one of the corporate behemoths. When asked how fashion had changed since the sixties and seventies, John B. Fairchild remarked:

The sad thing about fashion is that unless you have the backing of a big business machine, it is very, very difficult for a talented young designer to get started. And after they get started, they are never given enough time to prove themselves. With what it costs in merchandising and hype, it's extremely difficult for a designer to make a name for himself. Saint Laurent started with practically nothing and had to borrow money from an American used-car dealer to set up his house. That would be impossible today. The other thing is that these huge business machines don't get the message of fashion.... They limit the game to only a few big names, and the danger is the public will get bored.

Whereas previous fashion trends had made for memorable illustrations in *WWD*, the nineties represented a break with the past. The continuous presence of editorial art, which had been on the decline throughout the eighties, came to an end in 1991. Figurative illustration was deemed passé, and the task of interpreting fashion was relinquished to photography. In the end, *WWD*'s omission of traditional fashion art was as much a response to the popular culture as was the original inclusion. Reflecting the cyberaesthetic that had developed in the eighties, the elimination of fashion drawing represented a surgical excision of emotion in the publication.

The decline of editorial art was both regrettable and understandable. Bombarded for decades by photographic images in the media, the popular culture developed a reflexive predisposition for documentary representation. Exposure to virtual images on computer screens only reinforced the perceived authenticity of digital manipulation. In truth, digital editing rendered photographic reality a fiction. Historical figures and celebrities were raised from the dead for virtual cameo appearances in films such as *Zelig* and *Forrest Gump*.

By the nineties, the fashion industry was a well-oiled machine, with all of the players well rehearsed in their roles. No one had to be spoon-fed the next trend; the habit of gratuitous change and obsolescence was implanted in the consumer's psyche. A conditioned response to a set of visual cues was ingrained in the popular culture, and advertisers exploited this new way of processing visual information.[3] The instant messaging of photography was used to inspire consumer confidence in a predictable way. Photography was considered more accessible than illustration and demanded less of the viewer. With time considered to be the new currency, precious nanoseconds saved in immediate cognition had cash value. Gradually, viewers lost the ability to interpret the varying levels of abstraction in an illustration. The vernacular of fashion illustration had become too esoteric for the industry it served.

The overwhelming acceptance of photography as the visual language of fashion can also be attributed to the changing nature of garment design in the nineties. The affinity for basic silhouettes caused design innovation to become increasingly textile driven. Representing the experimental use of eccentric materials was a daunting task for the illustrator. Photography was better suited to the documentation of surface. Conceptual fashion designs, such as the ongoing metamorphosis of Martin Margiela's mold-infused garments, needed to be seen to be believed. It was now the photographer's challenge to selectively combine fact and fiction in accord

with the new cyberaesthetic. In this effort, the residual conventions of traditional fashion illustration carried over to photography. Location was used as a linking theme for multipage spreads. Props, gestures, and the interaction between figures conveyed narrative content. Extreme camera angles elongated figure proportion. The illustrative nature of digital compositing allowed photography to replace illustration as the unequivocal method for flattering the merchandise.

The diminished use of fashion drawing was also a ripple effect of the sixties' upheaval in the popular culture. Art, in general, became more interdisciplinary with the evolution of new communication formats. Fairchild archivist Merle Thomason said that she first observed the editorial preference for photography after *Blow Up*, Michelangelo Antonioni's thinly veiled biopic based on the life of British fashion photographer David Bailey was released in 1966. Before the sixties, illustration had been used to document haute couture. Beginning in 1912, hand-tinted plates were featured in limited edition fashion journals such as *La Gazette du Bon Ton*. Photography was historically relegated to the representation of mass-produced merchandise in mail-order catalogs. But the visual hierarchy was upended in the sixties when American ready-to-wear supplanted haute couture. Along with the fashion salon, the photographer's studio became an anachronism; Frank Horvat, William Klein, and Richard Avedon followed fashion into the street.

The sixties' inclusion of pornographic content in mainstream publications also had far-reaching effects. By the nineties, superstar photographers such as Meisel found new possibilities for subversion and experimentation. Anti-fashion statements served up a nihilistic slice of life with representations of heroin chic. Just about every taboo had been broken in the depiction of piercing, scarification, sadomasochism, and homoeroticism in fashion photos. Increased controversy seemed to speed the elevation of photography to the status of fine art.

As provocative editorial photography became the norm, illustration was no longer relied upon for what was once deemed the tasteful depiction of hosiery, foundations, and intimate apparel. The non-representational images of neoexpressionism left the editorial creative directors at a loss for the their next inspiration. A connection still existed between the fine and applied arts. Avant-garde fashion advertising took visual cues from high-tech Japanese anime and the primitive abstraction of outsider art. The idiosyncratic work of illustrators from other disciplines became all the rage in the fashion world. But the level of abstraction in manga and naive drawing did not satisfy fashion journalism's demands for specific information. And so, from 1990 to 1991, *WWD* continued to rely on a more traditional style of illustration before making the final transition to photography.

The fashion art from this brief period in the nineties represents a mature phase in the illustrators' careers. There was refinement of technique as opposed to radical innovation. Fast cuts and special effects in other media created a demand for even greater spontaneity and abandon in the art. The apparent immediacy may be attributed to the repetition of the task over a period of decades, but more likely to the artists' anticipation of dismissal.

With the absence of an illustration staff, the drawings that did appear in *WWD* after 1991 were of a different character. Fashion sketches that were the by-product of the design process were used to enhance the text. But such designer blueprints were far removed from the traditional role of fashion art as a commentary on the execution of an idea. In returning to a vérité format of fashion journalism, *WWD* had come full circle to the days when John B. Fairchild first took over as publisher.

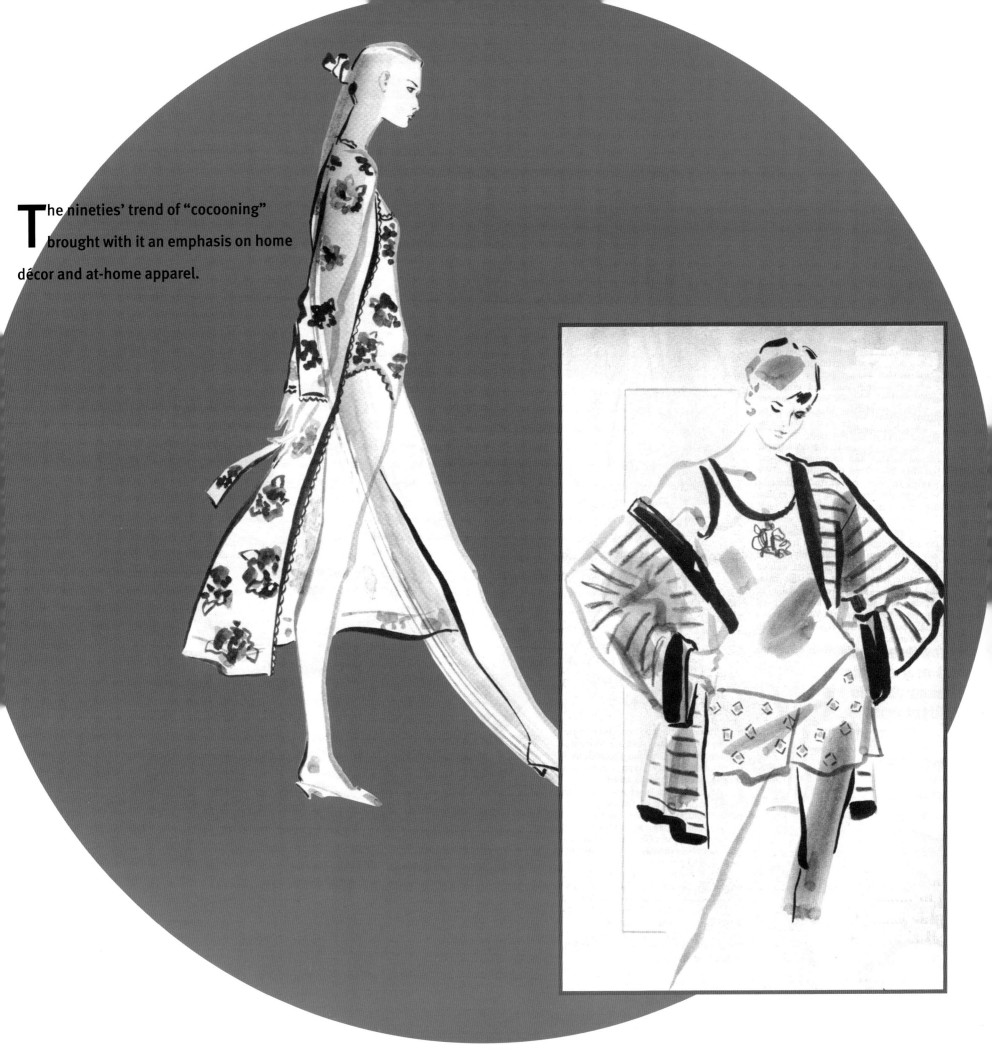

The nineties' trend of "cocooning" brought with it an emphasis on home décor and at-home apparel.

Robert Passantino's softened drawing style carried over to the nineties with the layering of transparent, fluid brush strokes. His elongated figure proportion is both ethereal and athletic.

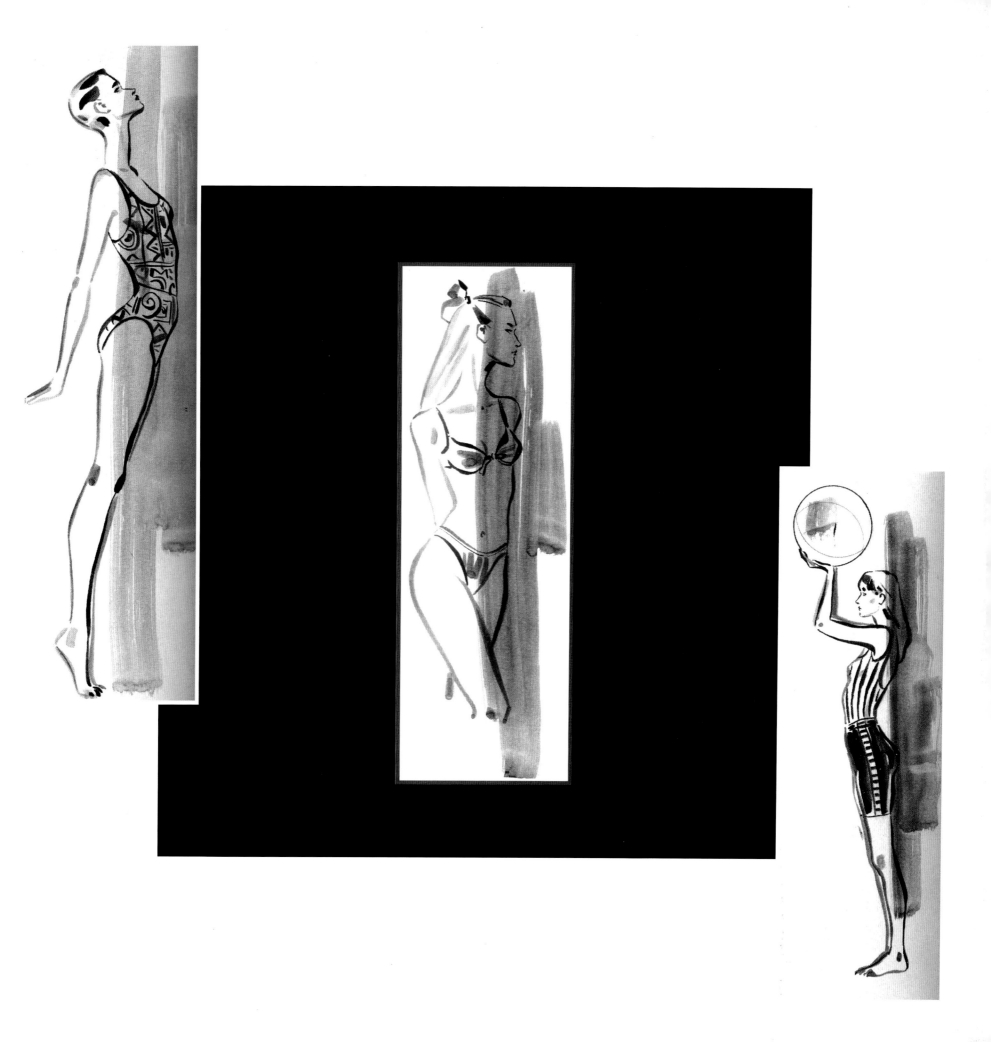

With the knowledge that their days were numbered, the *WWD* illustrators found a new context for presenting the latest fashion. The depiction of a politically correct high-fashion lifestyle in the early nineties was non-existent. In this illustration (*opposite*), by Kenneth Paul Block (Kenneth), both garment and fashion illustration were removed from the realm of status. It is interesting to note the reappearance of illustrations by Robert Melendez (*this page*), whose work had not been seen in *WWD* since the seventies.

The ultimate French Fashion Victim

CHLOE
*"It's a feminine
collection in
supple shapes,"
says Martine
Sitbon.*

**Martine Sitbon's
gray wool knit suit
with crystal buttons
for Chloe**

LANVIN
*"The collection is
inspired by the spirit of
Jeanne Lanvin," says
Eric Bergere. "It's for
an energetic
businesswoman who is
also a mother and a
passionate explorer full
of fantasies."*

**Eric Bergere's multicolor
linen tunic dress
with striped scarf
for Lanvin**

**Romeo Gigli's indigo
blue cotton lace and
organdy dress
with feathers**

RYKIEL
*The silhouette is
lean for spring at
Sonia Rykiel
with long knit
jackets over short
skirts in vibrant
colors.*

**Sonia Rykiel's
deep red wool and
angora skirt, tunic
and wool jersey
shawl collar jacket**

GIGLI
*There's an eccentric
edge to Romeo Gigli —
in strapless dresses with
jagged hems or in
cotton lace.*

O ccasionally a single, large, graphic image appeared on the cover of a supplement dedicated to a specific market segment. More often, tiny spot illustrations scattered throughout the paper were relegated to the task of mere decoration.

DRAWINGS BY KOCHISABURO OGAWA

NEW YORK — The newest crop of unitards plays u[p] the practical side of bodywear for fall. Cropped sh[orts] with tank tops, they have stretch appeal and allo[w] plenty of room for the active life. Details in design make a difference, as colorblocking and slimming stripes give the unitard an updated look.

Bod Squad

With a new focus on longevity, activities such as weight training, jogging, and martial arts were key to maintaining good health and a youthful appearance. In this two page spread, Kenneth Paul Block (Kenneth) used large cropped figures, which spilled over the boundaries of the picture plane.

eft, Marika's cotton
cra spandex unitard
sia and gray;
s light blue mock
eck unitard in
nylon and Lycra;
or blocked cotton
cra unitard from
namics in black,
and turquoise;
nikov's cotton and
striped unitard in
and white

S teven Stipelman's expert rendering emphasizes deep color without obscuring garment details.

RAWING BY STEVEN STIPELMAN

LES COPAINS

At Les Copains, spring-summer's simple and elegant shapes are enhanced by luxurious fabrics like cashmere, extra-fine wool, silk, wool gabardine and crepe.

Gold buttons and lace embroidery detail shirts, skirts, pants and jackets.

Blue dominates the collection. With red, white and gold it carries a marine mood. With yellows, greens, browns, and oranges it reflects the Tuscan countryside. Red, gold and rich bronzes are also key.

Ruffles and flounces, popular in the eighties, were scaled back for nineties' lingerie. Stipelman's selective broad brushstrokes offset the delicacy of the floral peignoirs.

SHORT AND SASSY

NEW YORK — Baby dolls are being cast in every short fashion story this season, but where they really belong and look their best is in the boudoir.

J.G. HOOK's sleeveless style swings into action in a floral cotton knit with lace touches (left).

BORDEAUX's cap-sleeve baby gives the empire shape a boost in a pink-on-white flower-print cotton knit.

Kichisaburo Ogawa's faces take on the appearance of masks worn in traditional Japanese theatrical performance. Similar in purpose to Noh masks, the neutral expression of Ogawa's faces relies on stylization to represent character.

SHADES OF WHITE

FALL
1990
Supplement to
Women's Wear Daily

WWD
INNERWEAR

Satin Dolls

Continuing from the eighties, luxe romanticism was given a new twist in the nineties. Pared-down silhouettes in satin crossed over from lingerie to the all-important slip dress.

Milan Gets Ready

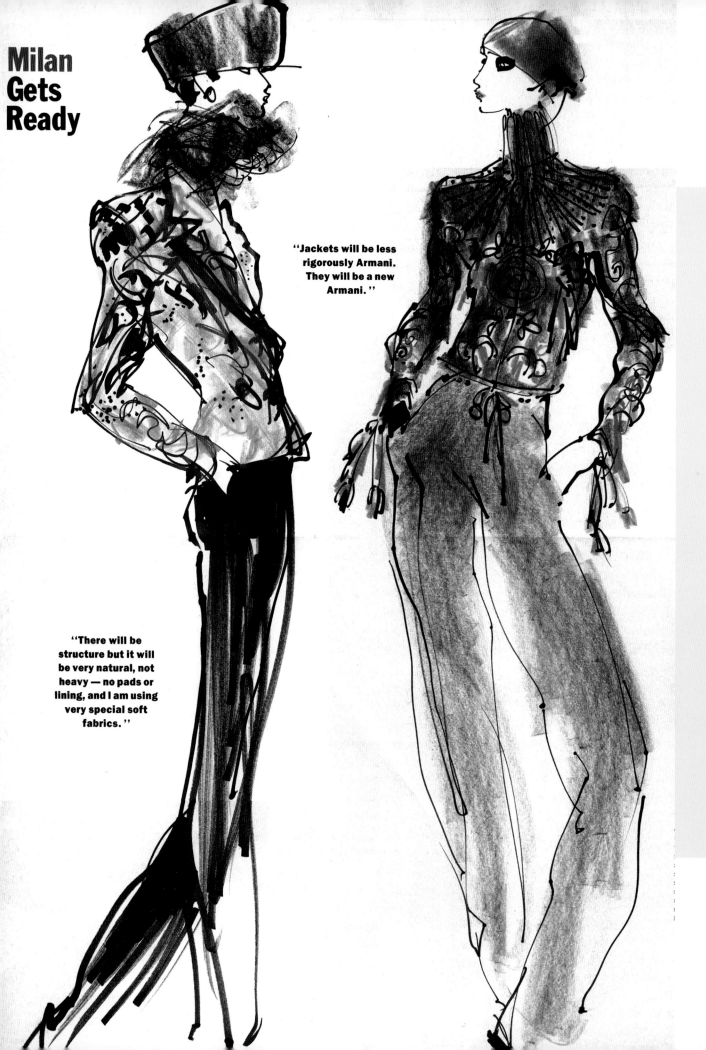

"Jackets will be less rigorously Armani. They will be a new Armani."

"There will be structure but it will be very natural, not heavy — no pads or lining, and I am using very special soft fabrics."

In a little more than a decade after the first Alta Moda fashion exposition in Milan, Italian designers such as Gianfranco Ferre, Alberta Ferretti and Georgio Armani became well established in the global fashion arena.

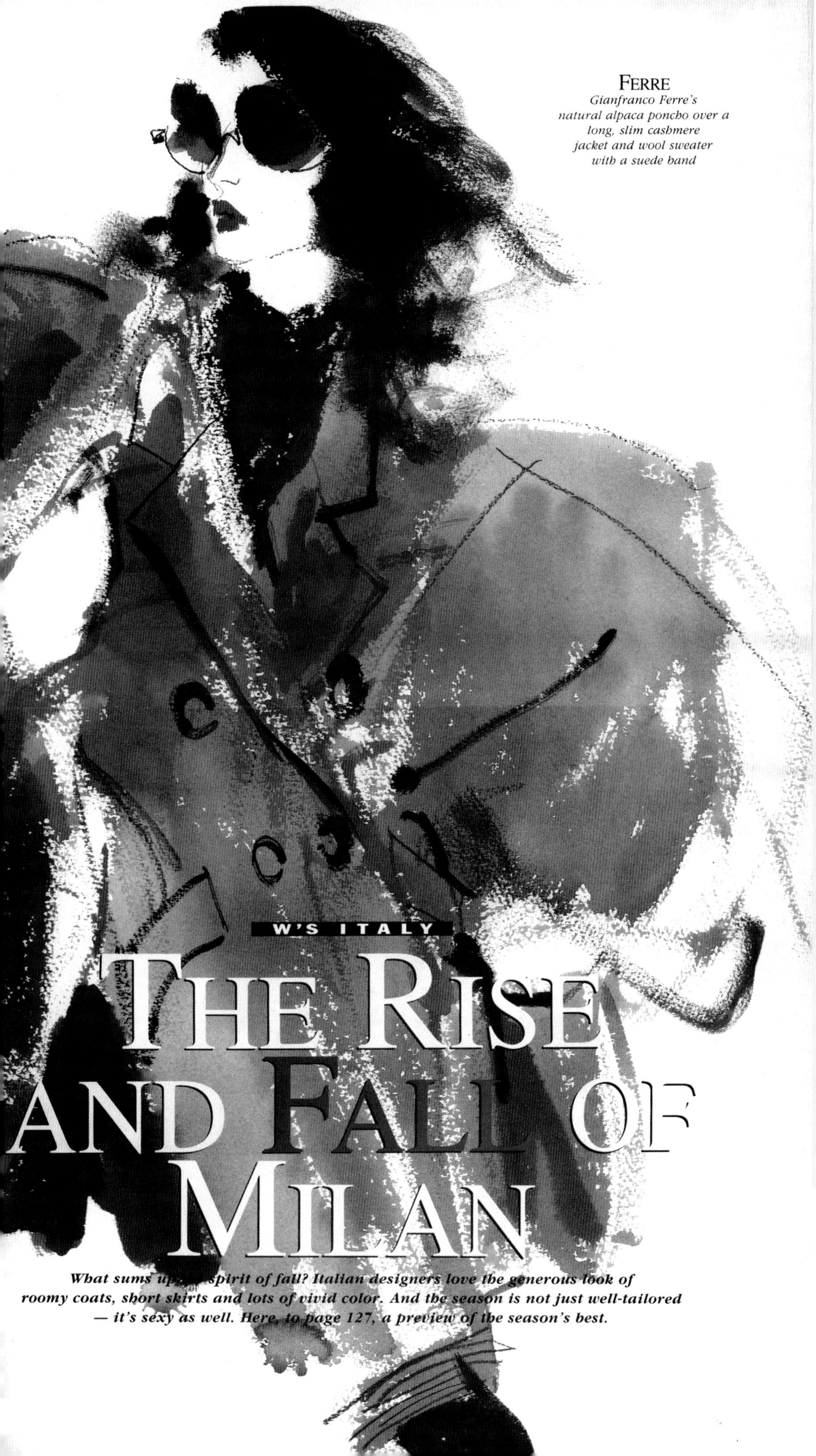

*Gianfranco Ferre's
natural alpaca poncho over a
long, slim cashmere
jacket and wool sweater
with a suede band*

W'S ITALY

THE RISE AND FALL OF MILAN

*What sums up the spirit of fall? Italian designers love the generous look of
roomy coats, short skirts and lots of vivid color. And the season is not just well-tailored
— it's sexy as well. Here, to page 127, a preview of the season's best.*

Kenneth Paul Block (Kenneth) used vivid transparent color to describe the bold, jacquard patterns of knitwear from Milan.

GENNY
Genny's print wool cape coat over slim wool leggings

FERRAGAMO
Ferragamo's wool and cashmere stripe coat over a merino wool knit jumpsuit

GIANNI VERSACE
Gianni Versace's baroque print wool ottoman suit

THE RISE AND FALL OF MILAN

KRIZIA
Mariuccia Mandelli's roomy wool tweed coat with a patchwork velvet lining over a wool tunic and knit wool ribbed tights for Krizia

W

the american way

The clean and simple shapes of American basics had global appeal in the nineties.

NEW YORK — Whether going for a gentler palette or clear brights, SA designers look all-American for spring in shapes that are clean and simple. You can always count on Oscar de la Renta to add lots of dash and drama, as in this sweeping evening coat — a striking swath of silk faille, with an iridescent silk chiffon blouse, cowl and wool crepe skirt.

ILLUSTRATION BY KENNETH PAUL BLOCK

46

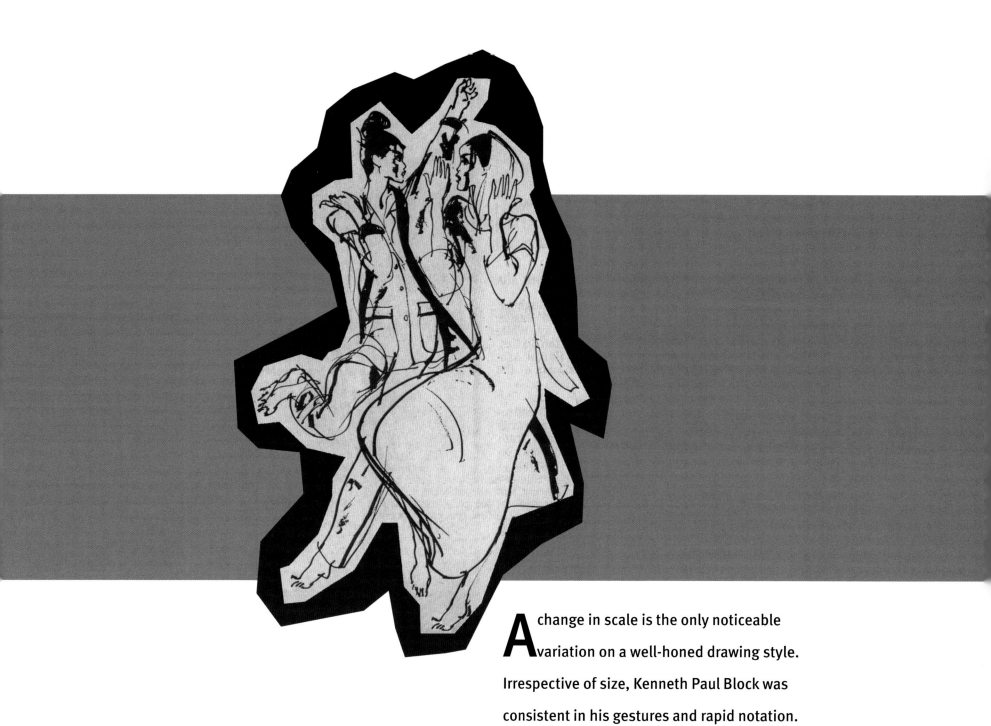

A change in scale is the only noticeable variation on a well-honed drawing style. Irrespective of size, Kenneth Paul Block was consistent in his gestures and rapid notation.

The Not-So-Naked City

Big black glasses

Khaki water-proof silk poplin parka revers-ing to ranch mink, lots of pockets to hold every-thing; navy cashmere and Lycra unitard

All About Hidden Luxury

Navy cashmere crewneck – to layer

Chocolate suede thigh-high boots — flat for ease

Chocolate croc back pack with change of shoes and overskirt in it

Michael Kors

Gold leather overskirt for evening

Gold leather ankle boot — walkable evening shoe

Donna Karan

After the dismissal of the art staff in 1991, there was the occasional appearance of designer sketches in *WWD*. In September of that year, *WWD* polled these top designers for their impressions of "the quintessential New Yorker."

Christian Lacroix

Karl Lagerfeld

Issac Mizrahi

The Quintessential New York Woman

Marc Jacobs for Perry Ellis

Marc Jacobs and Michael Kors portrayed the New York woman as a fashion follower constantly on the go.

NOTES

1. In her observations about macro trends in contemporary society, Faith Popcorn declared time the new money. Available at: www.faithpopcorn.com.
2. "Cocooning" is the term coined by Faith Popcorn to describe "The need to protect oneself from the harsh, unpredictable realities of the outside world." Available at: www.faithpopcorn.com.
3. Neal Gabler, "The Illusion of Entertainment," *The New York Times,* 4 August 2002, pp. 1–3

Women's Wear Daily • The Retailers' Daily Newspaper • December 13, 2001 Vol. 182, No. 114 $1.75

WWD THURSDAY

Sportswear

Street Scene

NEW YORK — Ripped and torn denim is back, and the East Village is the perfect setting for the casually dishevelled look it represents. New York artist Daria Deshuk, who painted the scene here from a WWD photo, managed to capture both the vitality of the city streets, and the laid-back vibe of the latest trend in denim for spring. "As an artist, I am a voyeur, stealing selectively from my immediate environment," she says. Here, her rendering of D&G's cotton denim jacket and skirt. For more, see pages 4 and 5.

Fortunes & Flagships: Retail Temples Rise Despite Recession

By David Moin

NEW YORK — Austerity measures? When it comes to building designer flagships, there's not much cutting back, not even in this down luxury cycle. Store costs are running high and designers and the corporations behind them are willing to foot the bill to be here. Prada's 30,000-square-foot SoHo store, opening Dec. 15, tops the charts. Estimated cost: $25 million to $30 million. More than a mere flagship, it's a work of high tech wizardry, created by architect Rem

See The, Page 10

"Fashion needs new names and excitement. It needs for the underdogs to bark."

John B. Fairchild (2001)

Epilogue

In the 21st century, there is occasionally an isolated opportunity for freelance art in *WWD*. But, more often than not, issues without illustration are the norm. The resurgence in popularity of figurative painting by Lucien Freud, Eric Fischl, Alice Neel, Chuck Close, and Philip Pearlstein will hopefully cause a corresponding revival in fashion illustration. Select department stores are already returning to the tradition of the illustrated advertisement. Shorter download times and an emphasis on animation make illustration a natural for the Web. Because digital imaging now allows photographers to create a total fiction, it is difficult to say where photography ends and illustration begins. With savvy readers beginning to reject photography as fact, magazines increasingly are using hybrid images in their editorial and advertising content. It may be only a matter of time before discontinuous change and the cyclic rejection of technology cause fashion illustration to appear brand new.